It All Began When...

LARRY WHITE

It All Began When...

Copyright © 2024 by Larry White

ISBN: 979-8989686377 (sc)

ISBN: 979-8989686384 (e)

Riverview Press

info@riverview-press.com
www.riverview-press.com

This book is in honor of
William Thurmond White.
His devotion to the Lord Jesus Christ made it possible for
this book to be written and published.
Whatever good results from this work are to his credit.

Contents

Introduction

Did you ever go into a McDonalds (or some similar spot) and see a group of seniors, usually men, drinking coffee and talking? Did you ever wonder what they talk about, especially if you see them there about every time you go in? I am a senior male and I've wondered, since I have never joined such a group. But I can guess. I suspect the number one topic is aches, pains, and prior surgeries. (That topic usually happens when I get together with another old codger.) They also talk about weather, sports, politics, and the economy. And I suspect, despite what Randy Travis sang, that it wasn't just old women who talk about old men; I'm sure old men talk about the women as well.

But depending on how long this group of seniors has been together and how comfortable they are with each other; you are bound to hear stories from their past. And quite possibly the same stories told over again and again. Like fishermen's tales they even only grow more embellished with each telling.

I resonate with the words of Psalm 111:2; "Great are the works of the Lord; they are pondered by all who delight in them." If you want a glimpse of Heaven, you can find it in that verse. For an eternity we will just enjoy hearing and telling stories of God's works in our lives and never tire of them.

This book is my attempt to get a bit of a head start on that endeavor. At the urging of several of my friends who have heard my stories, I have decided to write them down. For the sake of remembering the works of God you can join me in pondering them and delighting in Him. My ultimate hope is it will spur you on to expect God to work in your life as well.

And you will risk obedience to allow Him to show up.

It All Began When…

1948

Every story has a beginning. Whether it was "once upon a time" or "in a galaxy far, far away," there must be a beginning. Often a beginning is not easy to determine since most stories only build off another story. But as a storyteller it is necessary to determine what the starting point is for the story you are telling.

I have decided to begin my story about 20 days before I was born. That would be somewhere around November 24, 1948, in the little town of Westminster, South Carolina. It was the day before Thanksgiving.

I learned about this evening in detail from my 93-year-old dad a few months before he passed. He told me that he came home that evening after his shift at the local cotton mill feeling a weight of self-doubt. He was soon going to be a father for the first time, and he certainly didn't feel up to being a good father. It wasn't so much about his ability to provide, even though his salary as a laborer in the mill would not have been much. It was an overwhelming sense of inadequacy for the looming task. To be precise, he felt badly about his smoking habit, as he called it. (Since I was snugging in my mother's tummy, I was oblivious to how long he had smoked or how much he smoked). Dad was certainly not at all comfortable that he would meet this newborn with him having such a "filthy habit."

Dad's own father was a man who had been reprehensible as a father. He had been a cruel and very unstable figure to his family of 13 children and had abandoned them when the older boys were able to fend for themselves. I guessed, as I got old enough to think it through that my paternal grandfather was an alcoholic. I learned at my own dad's funeral that he was not an alcoholic, but a very cruel and argumentative man. My aunts told me that he did take his family to church but would find some issues that he found objectionable and would uproot them and move on to the next congregation, only to do it again. Based on the stories my father told me about his home life, that negativity and harshness was also manifested by Grandpa White in their home.

My dad escaped home as soon as he could, and eventually joined the Civilian Conservation Corp followed by an enlistment in the Army. He went on to fight in the European theater during World War II. He talked little about that experience except to show me the shoulder wound that took him out of commission. He often talked fondly of his time in Switzerland, and longed to go back someday, but mother disliked travel so they stayed put even after they could afford it.

Mother's family was a large, poor family that lived on mostly farmland that they cultivated. Her dad was given to wanderlust; so annually he would uproot the whole family and head from South Carolina to Florida never mind what this would do to the effect on her education. Not long prior to her marriage to Thurmond, my mother ended her formal education in the eighth grade. Her family was far more stable than my dad's, and the stability came through their commitment to their church-The Wesleyan Methodist Church.

As you can well guess, it was my mother's influence that prompted my dad to take the step he took that Thanksgiving eve. He got down by his bed and prayed, telling God he was not fit to be a father. He wanted to be free from smoking. He prayed that if God would deliver him from tobacco, he would serve Him for the rest of his life. It must have been more of a plea than a bargain because my father said, "When I got up from my knees, God took the craving for cigarettes from me and I have never desired to smoke again."

I was born on December 15. Ironically, it was my paternal grandfather's birthday. That was a Wednesday. I wouldn't be at all surprised that the following Sunday, December 19th was my first time attending church. Growing up meant church services every Sunday, both morning and evening services. Then Wednesday night was a prayer meeting. And revival services came both spring and fall. (I thought that must be what King David meant when he said, "…I will dwell in the house of the Lord forever." Ps 23:6)

Our whole world pretty much revolved around church. I loved Vacation Bible School each summer and I diligently did my scripture memory, but I was far from being as good as an older boy name Buddy Marchbanks, who later became a doctor. Our piano teacher, who was fondly called Sister Stubbs, felt I had a penchant for piano and gave me free lessons from first grade to seventh grade when I emancipated myself from the weekly grind of lessons. I very rarely practiced. I did get it so that I could play hymns, but nothing as good as Buddy Marchbanks.

Looking back, the discipline imposed by my church was rather stringent by today's standards. Mom and Dad took it seriously, so for them they never wore jewelry. In fact, it was not long before my mother's death in 2008 that I learned that she regretted that she never had a wedding ring. Dad, for the longest time, refused to wear a tie. His reasoning was, "If women can't wear necklaces because it is worldly adornment, then I won't wear a tie."

Most of the rules seem to target the women, but certainly there were those that affected me. We didn't have a T.V. until I was 13, but we did have nightly "family altar." It was mostly reading the Bible and prayer, but I remember the time my dad read to my sister and me, Uncle Tom's Cabin.

I was an average student, but my escape was books, either being read to or mostly reading myself. "Worldly" activities were frowned upon. I thoroughly enjoyed Halloween and chaffed when fall revival was scheduled at the same time. Fortunately, sports really didn't interest me, even though they were not strictly prohibited, except on Sunday.

My first time to attend a movie was at age 16. I was able to drive, so I took in "Lt. Robinson Crusoe" with Dick van Dyke. What I remember the most was the guilt and fear I struggled with worrying that Jesus might come back while I was in the theater. I wasn't sure, but I guessed I would go straight to Hell. (That was a subject I heard about a lot at revival services). When I got home from my first movie, Dad asked me, "Have you been to a movie?" I could not lie. I said, "Yes." All he said was "I am really disappointed." I certainly didn't like disappointing my dad, but based on his response I interpreted it as tacit permission. By then I was working and handling my own money, so movie attendance became a regular part of my life.

Along with movies I also got into enjoying rock and roll. I bought my own records and often pretended to be a radio disc jockey as I played them. I discovered live music (and dancing) at a local hang-out called, 'The Chicken Shack." Many a Saturday night you would find me there. And, when there were live concerts at nearby Clemson University, I would go. I saw such notables as The Four Seasons, Dion Warwick, and Roger Miller. But my most memorable concert was when I and two of my white buddies learned that James Brown was performing at Myrtle Beach High School. We were the only whites in the audience, and we had a blast.

There are so many memories about which I could go on, but in keeping with the theme of this book, I must answer the question, "Where is God in relation to me?" I often wrestled with that issue. I had heard a lot about Him, but except for one memorable occasion, to me He was the one who was dogging me with uncertainty and guilt. That one occasion was when I was 6 years old and at a revival service, I heard a stirring message on God's love. Evangelist Clinton Young preached such a convincing message about God's love for me that I "went forward" (a term used in the church to indicate going to an altar to pray at the front of the church and it was associated with someone seeking something special from God, like salvation). At the altar I cried rich tears of gratitude and release that God loved me.

But that experience was soon swallowed up by the ongoing struggle to live what I was told constituted a holy life, one pleasing to God. I never got the impression that God's love was anything but quite conditional. For Him to love me involved keeping a long list of negatives that collided with competing values that were increasingly coming at me as I grew older. How could God love me when I was resistant to my parent's expectations on me? How could He love me when I at age 12, made the intriguing discovery of sex. (I read up on the topic in the large medical manual in the family library). That knowledge opened me up to so many other new temptations.

Just to hang on to some hope of His love, I continued to go to church, even led in the youth group, avoided drinking, and certainly I did not smoke.

Yes, I was my church's youth leader. It was a result of showing up and that Buddy Marchbanks didn't. (I guess he was studying or practicing piano during that time). I proved to be creative in coming up with programs that engaged the group, but only two remain in my memory. The one I am ashamed of is the evening we got into a big debate over whether a person who is not a Christian can go to Heaven. I took a position that a sincere person stands a good chance in Heaven no matter religious beliefs. But the issue should have been, "Is Jesus the only way to heaven?" If my opponents had taken that tact, I would have had little to say. In my mind, I couldn't fathom what I knew of Christianity being an exclusive prerequisite for Heaven.

Another youth program I presented was also controversial. After Martin Luther King was assassinated, I was so moved that the next time our youth group met I read, "A Christmas Sermon on Peace." (Christmas 1967). My goal was to demonstrate that King believed pretty much what we believe. This was met by silence. I knew it was not a positive quiet.

20/20 Hindsight

Why was I so blind to the truth of God's unconditional love? I had heard John 3:16, "For God so loved the world that He gave His only begotten Son, that whoever believes in Him should not perish but have everlasting life." But I couldn't see that applying to me.

Mrs. Freeze

It all began when Mrs. Freeze, my English Composition teacher asked me, in a personal conversation, "What do you plan to be in the future?" I quickly replied, "A radio disc jockey." I was not prepared for her response. Mrs. Freeze looked at me with sad, but kind eyes and simply said, "That would be such a waste."

Had she not realized I wrote a regular column in our school newspaper on popular music? Hadn't she overheard me when I bragged that I was going to interview The Four Seasons when they came to perform at Clemson University? (That interview never materialized because they got lost trying to find the Field House and were 2 hours late for the concert). Didn't she realize I was trying hard to make a name for myself as the resident expert on popular music? Since I didn't play sports, that was my claim to fame.

When she pierced me through with her brief comment, I don't remember saying anything back to her. But I thought about the packet of information I had stored away in my room for the Columbia School of Broadcast. Granted, I had no real plan as to how I was going to afford to go to that school, but having the information fed my dream. Besides, I was only a junior and had plenty of time to figure that out; so, I thought.

It wasn't long after that conversation Mrs. Freeze brought to our class Dr. Paul Wood, a psychologist who taught at nearby Central Wesleyan. (Mrs. Freeze's husband was also a professor there.) I don't know what his talk on dream research had to do with English Composition, but I found him intriguing as he described the sleep studies they were conducting. Mrs. Freeze made a deliberate point of introducing me to Dr. Wood and he invited me over to the college to observe their research. In hindsight, I highly suspect all of this had to do with nudging me to Central Wesleyan since I attended a Wesleyan church in a community highly dominated by Baptists. Could it also be a subtle way of pointing me away from my hopes of becoming a disc jockey? If that was the scheme, it worked. I did act on the invitation to observe the sleep study. I certainly didn't understand it, but it appealed to my desire for the mysterious world of dreams.

I got further acquainted with Dr. Wood who I felt was a credible Christian. In addition, the campus of Central Wesleyan was conveniently only 4 miles from my house. I could continue to work and pay my way as I lived at home.

It all seemed to fit together as I ended my senior year of high school. I knew my parents would be pleased since their income wouldn't allow for funding my attendance as an on-campus resident. Nor were my grades scholarship worthy. Grant it, I felt a bit embarrassed when fellow students asked me why I was not going to Clemson? My answer: "Central is known for its Psychology Department." I would then quickly add, "I will probably transfer to Clemson after a couple of years."

When classes began in the fall of 1967, I was working part-time in a textile mill and had the money to buy the books and pay for tuition. I loved the freedom of driving to work and then on to classes. I even enjoyed the classes and took in the daily chapel services. Some were good and others, not so good. Good had to do with what spoke to me.

I also threw myself into the political campaign taking place for the 1968 vote. I got involved with The College Republicans and became The State Recording Secretary. That required my monthly attendance with other students at a meeting at the state capital. I felt what I was doing was very challenging and important and I appreciated the connections it was opening to me. In my mind I was a big man on campus even though it was a student body of about 400. At Central I felt I was somebody while at Daniel High School I felt like I was a nobody.

I learned how to fit in with those who were serious about their religion, and I felt like I was gaining approval with those whose focus was predominantly secular. I had picked up the habit of cussing with the crowd who cussed but I was successful in cutting it off when that was not appropriate. I didn't see it at the time, but I had become a big-time people pleaser. But I had a love/hate relationship with myself.

By the time my sophomore year rolled around, I was so into "fitting in" that the idea of transferring to Clemson had virtually disappeared. I loved where I was on so many levels. There were moments when I was bothered that I was so hypocritical. But I really didn't know the way out of it.

I genuinely looked forward to the Spiritual Emphasis week coming up in April on Campus. (Notice, it was not called spring revival). The speaker was Derric Johnson from Skyline Wesleyan Church in San Diego. What I sensed was that large congregation extended to me a hope of discovering a way of relating to God that was liberating from the pressure to perform religiously.

When Derric came, I was not disappointed. He talked about God loving us. His energy and positivity underscored his

9

message. I remember him sharing stories of individuals around Skyline whose lives were changed by Jesus as they encountered His love. He spoke at chapel every day and I was required to attend. I was happy to do it. Then he spoke every night. Since I was a commuter student, nighttime attendance was optional. But with Derric speaking, I didn't want to miss a word.

On Thursday night I could hardly wait. Pastor Derric's text was Jesus' words found in Matthew 11:28 "Come to me, all you who are weary and burdened, and I will give you rest." I remember little of what he said about the passage, but I knew I was weary. It is hard work to live your life trying to please people. And the alternative was clear: come to Jesus and learn from Him. That evening he did not issue a call to the altar, instead he explained that by praying and inviting Jesus in my heart, right where I was seated, I could begin a relationship with Him. I recall the prayer admitted to God that I was a sinner. It expressed gratitude to Jesus for dying on the cross for my sins. Then there was an invitation to him to come into my life and a commitment to follow Him as I chose to let Him lead my life. I was so ready to surrender my life to Him. That was exactly what I did that night.

Then there was an altar call. It was an invitation to come forward and thank God for answering my prayer. I was one of two students who responded to that invitation.

Repentance is a key component of conversion. How did I repent? Certainly, in my mind when I confessed being a sinner, my foul language was an issue. But far more significant than that was a change of heart toward Jesus Himself. Prior to that evening, I sincerely thought my salvation was dependent on my effort to live a life I thought Jesus required of me. The new take was that my heart and mind were now focused on Jesus Himself. It was a yielding of myself to Him and anticipating that He would teach me what He wants from me. I switched from people pleasing to Jesus' pleasing.

Repentance is also a process of change. Over the next year I lost my appetite for active political involvement. It happened as I began to see that even though the group I associated with were more or less, in agreement politically, we didn't get along with each other. There was infighting and bickering, not so much over policies but over positions and power. That was disillusioning. How were we going to make a better world?

The first test of my new faith came two weeks later. I was at Physical Ed. We were playing softball, and I was assigned to the far-right outfield, a place where I could do little damage as one of the poorest players on the team.

Ron Shuman was up to bat. Everyone knew that Ron was one of the best hitters, so I was alerted to be ready. Sure enough, Ron hammered the ball high into the air headed right into my direction. I moved toward the ball as it missed my glove and plowed into my right eye. As I dropped to my knees the shards of glass from my spectacles broke. I saw the blood coming from my eye and hit the ground.

Despite the pain the words of Romans 8:28 came to mind. I had just learned it. "And we know that all things God works for the good of those who love Him, who have been called to his purpose." I was flooded with peace as I was subsequently driven to the eye doctor.

After examining the eye and covering it with a patch, he told me it was very likely I would lose sight in my right eye. I was not to remove the patch until he removed it for me a month later. All month I kept reflecting on the promise of Romans 8:28.

When the month was up, the doctor expressed a bit of surprise and satisfaction that I did not lose my eyesight as he had expected. And my spiritual sight was immensely stronger.

20/20 Hindsight

As I look back over my first 20 years of life, not only was I on a quest for love, but I was also on a quest for significance. Jesus's promise to give his followers an abundant life (John 10:10) speaks directly to that quest.

It All Began When…

Heart Invasion

It was a Friday night at about 11:00 P.M. It was the beginning of my junior year in college. I had gathered with several male students on the front of the men's dorm after saying goodbye to my date of the evening, depositing her at the women's dorm. I was not ready to go home and wanted some more fellowship. I hoped I might find it with the handful of guys hanging out on the porch.

I had only been there for a few minutes when two men from nearby Clemson University suddenly joined us, but they were not looking for fellowship. They were obviously inebriated and were set out to make fun of Christians. I had never seen anything like this. I wasn't troubled by it but intrigued. Even though they were drunk and lacked inhibitions, what would prompt these two to want to pester what they assumed were believers in Jesus? That truly was an assumption on their part; a student at a Christian college doesn't guarantee you are a follower of Christ. Up until a year prior, I was certainly not a Christian. Almost within minutes of their approach the little group of students faded into the dorm leaving a freshman named Randy and me to engage these vocal skeptics.

We paired off with Randy taking one and me talking with the other. His name ironically was Larry. He wanted to

13

ridicule the idea of Christianity being the only valid way to God. Now, that was somewhat familiar territory to me. Plus, we had just had on campus a very passionate minister named Lucian Behar, who provided a series of messages on witnessing. In my heart I took the tack that this fellow might very well have come here that evening with a deep longing to know God. I also was asking God to help me to speak to his deepest need. We talked for over two hours and his sobriety began to come around. Eventually, he looked at me with a true sense of sincerity and said, "I wish I had what you have."

I didn't know what to say next. I had never led anyone to Christ and all my experience with such things was in the context of a church service. There was no congregation on that porch to sing "Almost Persuaded." I tried to remember the instruction I had gotten from Rev. Behar. He modeled taking the Bible and going through verses leading to a prayer. I realized how little I knew about the Bible and how to find those verses, even if I had a Bible handy.

So, I said the only thing I could think of, "Why don't you come to church with me Sunday." I was almost relieved when he angrily refused. I wasn't sure this Larry would relate to what I knew of the church I was attending. I grew up turning in the hymnal to singing two verses of "For the Beauty of the Earth" or "Onward Christian Soldiers." I had a hard time seeing this guy getting into that.

That experience effectively turned into one of my first assignments from God. I was to pray for Larry fervently including asking that I might somehow run into him again. It became an incentive to visit the Clemson campus, which I rarely did. I really had no reason to. But it wasn't too much longer after this encounter that this all changed.

Partly in hopes of running into Larry again I found excuses to go to the Clemson Campus, only about a mile from where I lived. As a high school student, I often frequented that library. I visited it again to complete assignments. I also found myself visiting the several eating places on campus, but I never saw Larry.

During one of those visits I saw a sign advertising College Life, a meeting for students by students featuring relevant talks about faith in the life of college students. It was sponsored by Campus Crusade for Christ at Clemson. I noted the time and place. That next Sunday night I made it a point to attend.

At that meeting were sharp students singing very upbeat and contemporary songs about Jesus. There was a funny skit followed by a male student and a female student talking about how Jesus had changed their lives and how He helped them with their daily problems. It concluded with a brief talk about how to know Jesus personally and a prayer to receive Him into your life.

This was incredible. Not only did it speak to me but if I could ever find Larry, this would be the perfect setting to invite him to respond to his "I wish I had what you have." I made note of the next College Life a month away and I signed up for small group study. I was sold out for this group of students.

After that meeting my social life shifted from Central to Clemson. I even joined in for a prayer meeting taking place every morning at 7:30 in the campus chapel. I was not used to praying with others out loud. I did have a pattern of taking a walk at night in my neighborhood and talking out loud to Jesus, but I was not sure I could do that with a group.

But I was so pleasantly surprised at my first group prayer meeting. Unlike prayer meetings I had attended at church, prayer was not verbalizing long, loud petitions to God. Instead, each student when they prayed did so briefly centered around one topic. Others would chime in with "I agree, God…" or adding to that first prayer their thoughts and concerns. No one prayed loud or long. I doubt I prayed in that first meeting, but not long after, I began to get my "prayer feet." I talked to God as if I were talking to a dear friend and indeed that was what He was becoming.

In late February I came to Central's campus for an afternoon class. I had missed chapel that morning because I had to work. I made my way to my afternoon class and there was no class. I was so surprised. I waited a while until someone dropped by the empty classroom to tell me everyone was still in chapel. Revival had broken out in chapel that morning. I was unaware that there was a revival service scheduled at that time. Chapel was 9:30-10:00 and it was now 2:00 P.M.

I made my way to Folger's auditorium and sure enough many students were still there. There was praying and tears flowing. I learned that students had spontaneously stood and confessed sins and repented of their lethargy about the faith. This continued to late into the evening.

A group of students from Asbury College in Kentucky had come to Central to tell how revival had begun there and they brought it with them to our campus. A group of us guys separated out from the larger group to pray and soon the idea came to go to Clemson to take this spirit of renewal to the students there. They followed me to the Crusade group that were meeting for deeper Bible study and prayer.

My encounter with a Clemson student had turned into a burning desire to see God work and to work through me. That yearning was still unmet although I heard other students talk about introducing fellow students to Christ. How did they do that? Being used by God became a deep longing in my heart. I was being carried along for a spiritual ride of my life.

Very early in my encounter with Clemson Christians I met a student named Lee Adams. Lee was from Cordelle, Georgia. As we spent time together for reasons I don't recall, he gave me a cassette tape of a man named Tom Skinner. Because Lee recommended it, I listened and was moved by the testimony of the chaplain of the Washington Red Skins. As a young member of a black gang, he heard a radio broadcast saying that a relationship with Jesus would change his life. He was struck with the words of II Corinthians 5:17: "Therefore if anyone is in Christ, the new creation is come: the old is gone, the new is here!" This Harlem gang leader tells how he received Christ, and he was transformed.

Then Tom went on to talk about how Jesus reconciled whites and blacks. He traced the history of the tensions between whites and blacks. I was so intrigued by what I learned that I must have listened to his message 10 times. I was understanding why I grew up in going to a white's only school and Blacks (Negroes) were bussed across Pickens County to go to an all-black school. I understood that that separation allowed me advantages. That difference made it possible for me to start working after school, which began at 14. I sharply felt the injustice.

When the Civil rights movement impacted our community, having heard Uncle Tom's Cabin prepared me to be sympathetic to the plight of those in my community who lived totally separated from me, though not far away in what was labeld colored town.

20/20 Hindsight

Romans 8: 14 says "For those who are led by the Spirit of God are the children of God." I can see now but I didn't understand it then, God's Spirit was leading me.

It All Began When…

Myrtle Beach Weekend

My mother and sister decided to take a short break at Myrtle Beach-a five-hour drive away. I was invited to go along. In my mind my goal was to connect with the Campus Crusade group that was there for beach outreach. I reasoned, "people on the beach are relaxed and might be very open to hearing about Jesus." It would be there that I would deliberately seek to share my faith and hopefully lead someone to Christ.

I had learned that Crusaders had a tool that they used to communicate the gospel, "The Four Spiritual Laws." I obtained some copies for that very purpose. But I'll admit, I had never even bothered to read one of them. I was told that all I had to do was just read them out loud to the person I was wanting to share with.

So as my mother and sister went about their vacation, I set out to tell others about Jesus. It went horrible. The attempts I made were rather quickly aborted. People didn't seem to want to hear. When I tried to share with them "The Four Laws", every time I was cut short with some reason to not listen. For the most part people were pleasant, but not interested.

After a day of feeling defeated, I made my way to an ice cream parlor where Christian students with Crusade hung out.

With my dish of ice cream I sat across the table from a Virginia Tech student named Phillip Fee. After a brief conversation I told him about my miserable efforts to witness. I remember saying, "It just doesn't work. I guess it's just not for me."

He then produced a little blue booklet and asked me. 'Have you made the wonderful discovery of the Spirit Filled life?" I had seen the booklet, but I assumed it was just The Four Spiritual Laws in a blue rather a golden color. Apparently, I had not heard about the Spirit-Filled Life.

On my admission Philip asked me if he might present this little booklet to me. I agreed. The booklet illustrated that there were 3 kinds of lives: the natural man, the carnal man, and the Spirit filled man. After unpacking each of them for my hearing, I had to agree I was the carnal man. I had invited Jesus into my life, but I was relying on my own efforts to live the Christian life. It was evident that even my attempts to lead others to Christ was MY effort.

I learned that God sent us His Spirit to enable us to live a fruitful Christian life. Successful witnessing was a result of His Spirit working in and through us. Jesus said, "But you will receive power when the Holy Spirit comes upon you, and you will be my witnesses in Jerusalem and all of Judea and Samaria and the remotest ends of the earth." (Acts 1:8)

Here I was in the remotest parts of the earth, Myrtle Beach, South Carolina, trying to bring people to Christ through my efforts. That was not all; my life for a year and a half had been an emotional roller coaster. At times I wasn't even sure of my own salvation and insecurity was worse when I would sin. I was weighed down with guilt and shame. I didn't have a clue as to how to be free. My relationships at home were very tumultuous. I was moody and difficult to live with, especially toward my dad.

The focus on the Spirit-filled life caused me to see that my problem was a lack of true surrender to God in every area of my life. I was willing to live my life for Jesus on my terms, not His. He wanted me to turn every area of my life over to Him. His promise was to forgive me and to fill, control and direct me with His Spirit.

The little booklet, like The Four Spiritual Laws, contained an example prayer. Phillip read the prayer and then asked if I would like to pray that prayer right there in the ice cream parlor. I don't know if my cheeks burned red. It would not have been from embarrassment from what those around might think; but I was so ashamed of how I had been living so independently from God. Grant it, like many Christians I was doing so out of ignorance. But now I knew.

I told Phillip that I would pray as I walked back to the motel where my sister and mother were staying. After all, my prayer life had been practiced predominantly by walks along in the dark.

On that walk, I confessed how wrong I had been in trying to live my life for Him and not allowing Him to live in and through me. I confessed my arrogant and independent attitude toward my father. I asked God to fill me with His Spirit and take over my life. I asked Him to use me in whatever way he would choose. I wanted people to see Jesus in me and through me come to know Him.

That night I didn't experience anything particularly unusual. But I did sense a release that I had turned my life over to Him and He took over the process of changing me and using me.

The next day, I set out again to witness. I was trusting in God to lead me to someone who wanted to hear the gospel. There were those who did take the time to listen. That afternoon a high school student name David invited Christ into his life as I shared the gospel with him. I was so excited. I could hardly wait to go back to the ice-cream parlor to tell Phillip.

Reconciling with my dad was a huge obstacle. The thoughts of humbling myself before him seemed so daunting. A few weeks after asking the Holy Spirit to fill me, there was an altar call in my home church. I was able to tell my dad how sorry I had been in the way I talked with him and treated him. With tears pouring down my face I sought his forgiveness. We embraced and wept together. There was such a healing there that even though we sometimes disagreed on various issues, those disagreements were surrounded by love and respect.

20/20 Hindsight

The Holy Spirit introduces us first to Jesus and as we follow, we then encounter the One some call the shy person of the Trinity, the Holy Spirit, Himself.

It All Began When…

Myrtle Beach, Part 2

Around 10 P.M. Sammy Scott and I were traveling south on The King's Highway in Myrtle Beach. Readers- whiplash alert-The last chapter ended in Myrtle Beach and even though this one begins in Myrtle Beach; two years have elapsed.

During those two years with my involvement in the growing ministry of Campus Crusade for Christ at Clemson, I had seen so many great things happen with that student body. The group had grown as we prayed regularly for Jesus to be the most talked about subject at Clemson. And He was.

A great example of Jesus being a focus subject at Clemson came about when Jane Fonda visited the university with an open-air event directed toward ending the war in Vietnam. Approximately 1000 students sat in the amphitheater to hear her spiel. When she opened the audience for dialogue, I was the first to get her attention. With much fear and trepidation, I queried, "You speak as if it is possible for war to end forever. Jesus seems to differ with that idea. He spoke that war is a chronic condition brought on by the depravity of humanity." In response Ms. Fonda went into a rant about what a cool guy Jesus was, and He is certainly one who would stand for an ending of war and us humans living in peace. I wanted to rebut, but I noticed she turned her attention to the other side of the audience.

But the rebuttal came for that side of the audience when a fellow Christian was able to sight chapter and verse of Jesus's take on our human condition. Then another believer picked up the dialogue from there.

When Jane Fonda was met by the local press after her Clemson stop, she indicated that Clemson was different from other schools in that she was asked about the Bible. She admitted to having never read the Bible, but she stated that if we would read the Black Panthers' Manifesto, she would read the Bible. Jesus was indeed a hot topic at Clemson, and I certainly did my part to bring attention to his Name.

I was finding myself growing bolder and certainly more fervent in my passion to witness. That explains in part what happened on that drive down Kings' Highway in Myrle Beach with Sammy. Being paired with a fellow Clemson student certainly helped. After all, Jesus sent the disciples out in twos.

That evening was one of the most dramatic times I had experienced with God speaking to me. Sammy and I were on our way back from enjoying a wonderful sea food dinner in far north Myrtle Beach, when we passed a billboard that was well-lit. In the light, I saw out of the corner of my eye, a man sitting on a suitcase. He in no way had signaled to us, nevertheless, I knew instinctively that he somehow needed our help. Sammy was driving and I instantly told him that we needed to turn around and go back.

Naturally, he was puzzled. "Why?"

"I don't know. We just must go back to a man I saw sitting under the light of that billboard we just passed."

"Was he thumbing?"

"No."

"Was he in trouble?"

"I don't know; we have to go back to him."

So, we did. As we pulled up alongside the man, Keith leaned out of his window, he asked, "Are you ok?" The man raised up two bloody wrists exposing the damage he had inflicted on himself.

Immediately, we both jumped out of the car to assist him. Keith was far calmer than I was. I knew that Keith's brother had committed suicide by slicing his wrist. Why was he so calm?

We learned his name was Jack. Jack had been kicked out of his house by his wife. He didn't want us to take him to the hospital. Sammy readily accepted that decision. We talked to him about Jesus, and he opened his wallet and showed a Four Spiritual Law booklet. We learned that he had been praying the prayer over and over in the booklet.

What he wanted us to do was to take him back to his home. He joined us in the car and directed us back to his place. When we got there, we learned that his wife, Teresa, was not at home so we began to help him clean his wounds. Then Teresa came home. She was furious with us for getting blood all over her clean bathroom.

Sammy and I excused ourselves. Then, giving Jack the information as to where the two of us were staying, should he wish to find us, we continued down King's Highway amazed at what we had just been through. I asked Sammy why he had not been more forceful in getting Jack to go to the hospital. He told me that he knew, based on his experience with his brother, that Jack had not inflicted the kinds of wounds that were lethal, but he also knew that with a pair of scissors in his hand he was aiming in that direction. I realized that Sammy had gotten the scissors out of Jack's hand. Now I understood some of the reason Sammy had remained so calm.

We committed ourselves the rest of the evening to pray for Jack and Nancy. When morning came, we slept on through until about 4 that afternoon when we learned that someone was at the front door wanting to see us. It was Jack and Nancy, smiling, holding hands, and thanking us for what we had done. It was obvious that Jack's wrists were professionally bandaged and whatever wounds were there between them had also been patched up. We never saw them again.

20/20 Hindsight

So, God speaks to me! God spoke again at an ice cream parlor two years prior right in Myrtle Beach. Now he had spoken again.

It All Began When…

An Unplanned New Years Eve

I was facing New Years Eve 1971 with no plans. The past two New Year's Eves had been powerful experiences at Campus Crusade Conferences in Atlanta. Ballrooms with speakers and music and college students from all over the Southeast. Warm enriching memories that propelled me to new heights of devotion and zeal.

This year's conference was completed before the time New Years Eve came. Again, it had been in Atlanta and had been wonderful. Rather than bringing in the New Year as a part of the conference, this year's highlight had been going out from the conference center to share Christ. This was a usual part of any Crusade conference. You chose a partner (men always witnessed to men and women shared with women); then you were assigned to a part of the city where people congregate. I had partnered up with a student from the University of South Carolina named Mark. I had met Mark on a Jesus March at our state's capital, Columbia, earlier that spring. Students from campuses across the state converged to demonstrate our allegiance to Jesus.

As I marched along, I noticed another student who seemed to be a bit out of place. He was alone and seemed more interested in looking at the other marchers. He didn't carry a poster or plaque and didn't join in with the singing or chanting slogans. I felt drawn to him out of curiosity; after striking up a conversation with him, my assumptions about him were confirmed.

It turned out Mark was a sociology major at the University of South Carolina. He came to the march wanting to learn what sort of people would participate in a Jesus March. By the time we reached the steps of the State Capital to hear speakers, Mark and I were deeply engaged in a conversation about the gospel. Although pleasant, he was objecting to the message of Jesus's death and resurrection being relevant to people today. Other marchers overhead the conversation and joined into the discussion. Soon we were sitting on the sidewalk, Bibles were out, and Mark's concerns were being addressed by students quoting verses and sharing testimonies.

Mark listened and became increasingly responsive. I felt led to let others talk and I prayed silently for the Holy Spirit to open his blind eyes to the truth. His eyes were opened, and Mark that Sunday afternoon embraced Jesus as his Lord and Savior.

He and I continued to correspond by letter. He availed himself of the Crusade group on his campus. And he joined in for the annual Christmas Conference. And now we were partnering together in Underground Atlanta to tell others the good news. I felt so delighted that someone I had had a part in bringing to Jesus was with me.

But this New Years Eve itself appeared to be one that would be particularly lonely. Until I got a call from Judy*. Judy and I met at Central Wesleyan when she was a freshman, and I was a sophomore. I was attracted to her long brown hair and the enthusiastic energy. We dated toward the end of her freshman year. Then her second year, she decided that she could no longer afford Central and continued her education at the University of Alabama. She lived in Tuscaloosa and like me became a commuter student. We both made feeble efforts to keep connected.

Surprisingly, she called me and told me she was going to be back my way that New Year's Eve and wondered if we could get together. That suited me perfectly. We took in a movie and then we sat in a restaurant catching up. I'm sure I directed the conversation to my involvement with the Clemson Crusade group. Of course, I talked about the conference I had just attended. Certainly, I told her about Mark and Underground Atlanta. Then with the persuasiveness of a salesman, I talked about the upcoming Explo 72 in Dallas. I clearly remember encouraging her to go to Explo '72 in Dallas. It would be in June. She was not ready to jump on board.

One thing I strongly remember us saying to each other (even though I can't recall who initiated this part of the conversation) was that neither of us had met anyone else we would rather be with than each other. With that we agreed to be committed to pursuing an exclusive relationship despite the distance between us. It was some time afterwards that Judy decided to join me at Explo '72. I was so thrilled.

But rough waters were ahead. I took a summer job as a youth leader at St. Mark's Methodist Church in Seneca. Seneca was the town where in the fall I would be a teacher in the Jr. High School. From Judy's perspective things were lining up for marriage. We talked about it, but I was growing more and more aware that Judy did not share my excitement. I had a hard time labeling why she was not excited about the things that excited me. But when she agreed to go to Explo 72 with me, I was sure that experience would make a huge difference.

It didn't. In fact, it made it worse. Judy made it abundantly clear that she was opposed to the whole thing of witnessing to others. In the meantime, my commitment to evangelism was only solidified when I learned from a letter from Mark's sister that in a construction accident Mark had died. I grieved the loss, but felt so glad that I knew someone I had had a part in their conversion was in Heaven. Judy neither shared my grief nor my joy.

As I started in my work of teaching junior high students, Judy stepped up her conversation about marriage and I would say, "But I do want to join the staff of Campus Crusade," thinking she would come around. And she would say, "After we marry, we can consider that."

20/20 Hindsight

There are three good reasons people marry:

1. Love-a sense of belonging that brings warmth and caring.
2. Sex-both safe and regular
3. It's the normal, natural, right thing to do.

Considering I had come to the end of my college career, it was this last one that was taking precedence.

*Note: Judy was not her real name.

It All Began When...

"Thumbing" in Atlanta

I pulled my car into an Exxon station off Highway 20 in Aniston, Alabama. It was Friday evening, and I was on my way to Tuscaloosa when my Rambler started running hot and couldn't make it another mile. I called Judy* to come and get me 119 miles from Tuscaloosa.

The next Sunday afternoon, she returned me to the Exxon Station where I thoroughly thought I would find my car repaired and I could be on my way back to Freedom Drive in Clemson where I lived with 3 other men. Then I could make it the next morning to my job at Seneca Junior High where I taught. Well, that was not the scenario at all. The ailing car was still sitting right where I had left it Friday. What was I to do? The station promised to fix it and I had no choice but to leave it.

I noticed a middled age couple in a very comfortable car with Georgia license plates, filling their tank. I approached them with a prayer of "help" in my heart and they graciously gave me a ride for two hours to the top of Atlanta. As they let me out on Highway 85 North, the sun was beginning to set, and I knew my place in Clemson was another two hours away. Nevertheless, a great peace settled over my heart. I knew this was God's problem. He would solve it.

I took my one suitcase and began to walk up the interstate. I knew God was completely in control and I felt strongly that something remarkable was going to come out of what looked like a dire predicament.

I had not walked long up I-85 when a big Lincoln Continental pulled over and a man motioned me to join him. I noted that it had an Alabama tag. I met Mike and quickly learned that he was going to Clemson, South Carolina to work as a boiler maker at the Duke Power plant. He would be there for a week. God had provided a ride to my front door. But there was much more.

We had driven just a short distance when Mike reached across to the glove compartment and produced a bottle of Jack Daniels. Anticipating a two-hour ride, he was extending hospitality. I graciously declined and he wanted to know why. I responded, "I don't need it."

"What do you mean?" Mike asked.

I explained that two years earlier I had become a Christian and consequently, I really didn't have a need to drink.

This opened a very engaging conversation. This tall, married man, with little daughters, asked me question after question wanting to understand my statement about "becoming a Christian." Never once did I feel he was belittling me or ridiculing my claim to faith. He sincerely just wanted to understand. For the next two hours we talked nonstop. (It was one of those times when I would have loved to have had a recording of what I said.)

When he dropped me off at my front door I said to Mike, "It was no accident that you picked me up. Thank you so much for the ride. And Mike, this time was also for you. God was speaking to you in our conversation. You must decide what you are going to do with what you have heard. I want to come to your motel room Wednesday night and see what your decision is." He agreed.

Wednesday came and I made my way to his room at the Clemson Motel. I knocked at his door, and he called out, "Come in."

When I entered the room, he was laying on his bed with the Gideon Bible open in front of him. There were more questions.

Finally, I asked Mike, "What has happened to you since we last talked?" Mike said, "When I got to the room, I knelt by my bed and asked Jesus into my heart."

I was so aware we were in a motel and I'm sure the walls of Mike's room were not very thick, so I refrained from the exuberance I felt inside. Nevertheless, my expression of joy and satisfaction were genuine, just not very loud. And I was awed. This was almost like a story book in its climax. What started with a broken-down car ended in the salvation of a man who would grow to a dear big brother.

Every time Mike came to South Carolina we would meet and study the scriptures. If he wasn't coming my way, I would be driving close enough to tiny Ashland to stop, spend the night in Mike's home and have a study with not only him but Joan, his wife, who had also embraced Jesus. We were together at least twice a month.

In January, when I stopped to visit with Mike and Joan, I mentioned to Mike that Judy had expressed frustration with me. She didn't appreciate that I took her and my precious time together to be with him. I had given her an engagement ring for Christmas. I was confused by her lack of appreciation for the passion of my life.

Mike calmly looked at me and said, "You two don't seem to be on the same wavelength." That insight on his part startled me. Until that evening, I had never divulged Judy's misgivings. As a very young believer I was shocked at Mike's insight.

20/20 Hindsight

The old hymn says it best, "To be happy in Jesus, we must trust and obey."

It All Began When...

Valentines 1973

Valentine's weekend 1973 rolled around and found me again with Judy in Tuscaloosa. I brought flowers and looked forward to celebrating the occasion with my now fiancé. Undoubtedly, she would want to discuss the possibility of a June wedding. I came to the weekend pondering how my job I had teaching in a junior high school classroom had proven to be totally undesirable. I loved the kids but being confined in one place all day made me miserable. I just couldn't imagine doing it another year. To say I felt trapped was an understatement.

I had no plan to break it off with Judy, but much to my surprise, she carried out her plan to break it off with me. That included giving me back the ring I had given her at Christmas.

There was some relief but also some hurt. Immediately I got on the phone and called the University of Alabama Crusade staff and asked if they could arrange an interview with me for the purpose of joining the staff of Crusade. I was so pleased when they called me back and told me that they would interview me Saturday afternoon. Along with the interview they gave me the necessary application to take my next step.

As I returned to Clemson, I stopped in Ashland to tell Mike and Joan the news. I felt they saw it as good news, but I wasn't quite ready to go there. Rejection, even when it makes good sense, hurts.

I returned to the job that had become my albatross. Before filling out the application for Crusade staff I took a day alone with God and prayerfully did a pro/con chart. My two options were joining Crusade staff and staying on at Seneca Junior High for another year.

The pro for staying on was steady pay and familiarity with the location. The con for Joining Crusade staff was having to raise my own support. After all, I had paid my way through college. How could I possibly ask people to support me in doing something I so dearly loved doing? Besides, I was sure being on Crusade staff would take me to places I had never gone.

The con list for Crusade was greater than the pro list for Seneca Junior High.

But I filled out the staff application and mailed it in anyway. I would let God decide.

Six weeks passed since Judy had given the ring back. I waited, sort of hoping she would change her mind. But finally, I traded the ring in for some items I needed for the new life I was going to pursue, mainly an electric typewriter. It was a Saturday. That evening at about 10:00 P.M. I got a call from Judy. After some pleasantries she proceeded to tell me why she had called. "I wanted you to hear form me before you heard it through the grapevine—I am engaged to marry, and I wanted to not only inform you but invite you to the wedding."

I'm sure there was some space of stunned silence. Finally, I offered a halfhearted congratulations. Rejection always hurts even when you can rationalize the wisdom of it. I felt the full impact of her rejection. Then I asked, "Who are you engaged to?" "His name is Rick."

"Were you seeing Rick when we were dating?"

"No, but I knew him."

"When is the wedding?"

"June. Can you come?"

I honestly was flabbergasted and concerned for her future when I answered, "No, if all goes as planned, I will be going to my first staff training for Campus Crusade." I had not been officially accepted but I felt very confident I would be. I was so glad I had a legitimate out, even though it was tentative. I could not see myself going to her wedding.

After a quick goodbye, I went to my bed exhausted and numb from the phone call. I lay awake going over and over in my mind what had happened since Valentine's weekend. I could not quiet my mind. Finally, at 3:00 A.M., I turned on my light and prayed, "God give me something that will help me in my dark time here." Then I reached for my Bible and opened it, not sure where to look, it fell open to Psalm 128 and I read these words; ***"Blessed is all who fear the Lord, who walks in obedience to him. You will eat the fruit of your labor; blessing and prosperity will be yours. Your wife will be like a fruitful vine within your house; and your children will be like olive shoots around your table. Yes, this will be the blessing for the man who fears the Lord."***

I was amazed at the words I read. I went back and read them again, especially the promise found in verse 3: ***Your wife will be like a fruitful vine within your house; and your children will be like olive shoots around your table. Thus is the man blessed who fears the Lord."***

I closed the Bible and turned off the light. I fell into a very peaceful sleep.

20/20 Hindsight

Even employing a poor method of Bible study can sometimes provide God an opportunity to speak to our lives, if we are genuinely seeking Him,

It All Began When...

Staff Training Purdue

June 1973 rolled around, and I did not renew my teaching contract. I was left with a window of time before I was to report for my first staff with Campus Crusade training at Perdue University. From my connection with St. Marks Methodist as a summer youth leader the summer before and my teaching at Seneca Jr. High School, I had become known in the community. That resulted in being asked to help chaperone the high school band's trip to celebrate the 25th anniversary of Israel.

I was so happy to participate. I certainly saw it as an opportunity to evangelize not only the band members but also those who came to New York to celebrate the birth of Israel. I turned to my friend Lee Adams who was now on staff with Campus Crusade in Los Angeles. I asked if he could send me some Jews for Jesus broadsides. I had discovered they were easy to read and very to the point of the Gospel. I planned to distribute them along the parade route.

Lee graciously sent me 100. Frankly, I had hoped for more. Considering the multitude who lined the parade route, 100 would hardly suffice. So, I prayed that each brochure would find its way into the hand of someone who would read it and be impacted. I prayerfully began to pass out the literature as the band lined up on the parade route. I put myself at the rear of the band in front of a large group of marchers who were dressed in black uniforms. They were young and I had no idea that they represented the JDL (Jewish Defense League).

One of the JDL came up to me and asked for a broadside. I saw him step aside and read it carefully. Then he took it over to others who were his comrades. They gathered around and read it and as they did, they would look over at me. I noticed they were not smiling. Soon all of them had read that one brochure and there were easily 40 or 50 marchers.

I felt like God was clearly answering my prayer and I was thrilled! That is, until the leader who I had given the one piece of literature to came over and snatched the remaining broadsides out of my hand. He promptly shredded them, throwing the pieces on the ground and cursed me. "Why are you giving this Jesus stuff out at this parade?" He didn't wait for an answer but returned to the contingency he was a part of.

Somehow, they connected me with the high school band and began to taunt the high schoolers who had nothing to do with my activity. It wasn't long before someone from the parade Marshall got word to me. I was told that the JDL was one of the most militant groups in the city and I would be wise to lose myself in the crowd. And certainly, for the sake of the Seneca High School band, I complied as soon as possible. It was certainly the first time I had experienced persecution.

When I returned to South Carolina I then made my way to W. Lafayette, Indiana, the location of Perdue University where I was to begin my training as a Campus Crusade for Christ Staffer. The first Sunday I attend the Free Methodist Church, where the pastor welcomed the students and staff of Campus Crusade attending his church that summer. He invited us to participate in the church's ministry.

Three of us, including myself, volunteered to offer a special song during our stay. The other two were Pam Marx and Becky Edwards. We chose to sing a popular Bill Gather song, "He Touched Me", which necessitated practice. I played the piano, and we ran over the song numerous times anticipating our performance. Little did I realize that God was introducing me to the woman he promised a few months earlier as my "fruitful vine about my table."

The alto was Becky Edwards. She had joined the high school staff a few months earlier after graduating with a master's in early childhood education from Auburn University. She was a petite blond with a nice Alabama accent and a delightful sense of humor. Becky was born with a noticeable birth defect. Both of her arms were shorter than normal with her hands attached to the elbow joints. Nonetheless, I found her attractive both physically as well as an enticingly warm personality as we practiced. I was very intrigued by this warm unique woman.

After we sang for the congregation, she and I continued to meet to sing and pray together. After our staff training ended at Perdue University, we went our separate ways. I was assigned to the high school ministry in Austin, Texas, and she went back to her assignment in Jackson, Mississippi. We did exchange addresses, I think.

Let me indicate something quite noteworthy. I reported to my first Crusade assignment with full support pledged. I didn't raise it penny by penny. God graciously put together my support team and most of the funders were people I had met that year between graduation and staff training. While I had run to my "Tarsus" by being a teacher; he faithfully introduced me to churches and individuals who would join me financially for the next 14 years.

January there was a staff ski trip to Pueblo, Colorado. I signed up looking forward to my first time on the slopes and hopefully seeing Becky Edwards again. I had heard she was coming.

But much to my dismay she was a no show. I learned from other staff from Jackson that Becky had to cancel her trip due to the flu. I was surprised at the level of my disappointment (even more disappointed than I was in my poor performance on the slopes; I hardly managed the bunny slope). Even so, I compensated for my lack of snow skiing skill with snow tubing. I handled my disappointment with the absence of Becky by finding a get-well card and had everyone sign it, camouflaging my signature and my effort on her behalf.

That next summer staff training was shifted from Perdue University to Colorado State University in Ft. Collins. A year later after first meeting Becky, we connected again in Colorado. It surprised me how wonderful it was to finally see her again.

I had been promised that my wife would be a fruitful vine at my table. I don't know how I expected that woman to appear in my life. I had occasionally dated other staff women and enjoyed the time, but my inner reaction to Becky was telling. But just as the attraction was increasing, the hesitancy was equally as strong. Did God lead me to a woman who was born with a handicap?

20/20 Hindsight

It is not that men are less emotional than women. We are good at compartmentalizing our emotions and being surprised when they show up. I was becoming a student of myself by watching my reactions.

It All Began When...

A Single Person's Identity

I read a brief article entitled "A Single's Person's Identity." It was the summer of 1975, and I was headed to Colorado State for the annual Crusade staff training. The essence of the article was a reasoned appeal for singles to make overt commitment to friendships with the opposite sex based on unconditional love. It was written by John Fisher. It not only made sense to me, but it seemed like the clear way out of my inability to move forward with Becky.

We had our annual "date" that summer. It usually consisted of sitting down at a piano singing together, then catching up on our past year, followed by praying together. We would even do it a couple of times in our brief time together during the summer.

The second time we got together I suggested we go to a small local restaurant where you were served your steak and you were equipped to cook it on a grill right in the restaurant the way you liked it. I've never found such an arrangement since. It was fun.

Then as we downed our meal the subject of "A Single's Persons Identity" came up. I brought it up hesitantly, not sure how it would be received. She had read it and like me thought it was a great article! Before the meal ended, we made a commitment to an exclusive friendship. I felt like something significant took place and I was sure it meant deliberate action on my part. Particularly, I was to communicate with Becky by mail and phone on a regular basis. There was no such thing at our disposal as the internet.

Becky confided in me later that she felt nervous about her ability to follow through on the commitment. We were living busy lives. I was in Austin. She was now in Nashville.

As the year went on, I began to experience a growing desire to fly to Nashville and see Becky. I didn't want to wait until next summer to get together. So, on Easter break, I made my way to Music City. The week together included a visit to Florence, Alabama, to meet her folks, a visit to the Space Center in Huntsville and, attending an evening of comedy back in Nashville at the Peabody Campus. It was a very memorable time in many ways. We enjoyed so much our time together and the week ended way too soon.

But not too soon for us to talk about the summer 1976. My plan was to stay in Austin most of the summer to prepare our youth to attend a summer conference. The main task was organizing a huge garage sale. Her plans included participating in a summer beach project. She wasn't sure where. But we would see each other again at staff training at CSU.

The summer of 1976 was the celebration of 200 years of U.S. history, but it hardly went noticed by the two of us. I learned in May that Becky was assigned to a beach project in Galveston-226 miles from Austin. Becky asked me to pick her up at Houston Airport. Now that was a given. I was thrilled.

But I was puzzled. A staff member is given the option of three choices for a project. I knew that Becky had made her first choice as Panama City, Florida. Her third choice was

Galveston. It is extremely rare to be assigned to a third choice. Frankly, I had all but resigned myself to the fact that she would NOT be in Galveston. But I certainly had prayed that would happen. And it did!

When we were loaded in my car and on our way to Galveston, I turned to Becky and asked. "Why did you make Galveston your third choice?" She replied. "I did not want to be the one who put myself there knowing you would be so close. I wanted God to put me there." That answer satisfied me. To me it was a huge confirmation that God was working on bringing us together and I couldn't be happier. Clearly, she was a woman who trusted God.

Again, two weeks later I traveled to Galveston to spend time with this very special woman, and I was prepared to share with her an issue I had struggled with from the first time I met her. As we sat by the bay with the moon hanging low over the water, I took her hand and broached a very tender subject.

"I want you to know that I love you." I had clearly progressed from being a committed friend to being in love with Becky. I proceeded to say, "I don't know if you have ever wondered how I've felt about your handicap. I no longer love you in spite of your handicap; I love you even with your handicap. I just love you just the way you are."

She responded positively but a little coolly, I thought.

Later I learned that it really didn't hit her until later that evening what I had said and how perfectly it had addressed a huge concern she was harboring prior to connecting with me in Texas.

I spent that night sleeping on a trampoline in the gym of a church beside a window opened to the sea breeze. I slept like I was floating on a cloud all night, but I don't think the trampoline, or the sea breeze created the sensation. I think the new level of love I had expressed openly to my sister in Christ, my friend, and the woman I wanted to marry left me suspended in mid-air.

Becky later was able to come to Austin. I planned a picnic for the two of us in the Hill Country west of the city. It was a beautiful day, and the terrain of the hill country was so spectacular. I had borrowed one of the youth's old trucks to haul stuff for the garage sale. I bought Kentucky Fried Chicken (Becky loves fried chicken) and off we rode looking for a place for our picnic. I was surprised that this proved hard to find but eventually we came to a beautiful Episcopal church. It overlooked a great valley of green behind it and there were steps leading down from the upper level to a lower level. We adopted the stairs as our picnic spot. We sat and talked and talked and yes it was there that we first kissed, as I told her again that I loved her.

Time got away from us. While we were there, we were so lost in those moments that we had not even noticed that above us the church was filling up for a wedding. Suddenly, a man dressed in a tuxedo appeared at the bottom of the stairs and told us that we had to leave. I stood up and investigated the situation. I looked through the bottom of the huge window to see the activity taking place just over our heads. We scrambled to collect our empty KFC boxes and quickly made our way to the rough looking truck parked in front of the most elegant setting. It was just a part of a memory that so characterized our lives.

Had we discussed marriage? As the summer progressed, we certainly did. We felt it was God's plan for us, but the question was, when? We both felt we needed more time together before that step. As we headed to staff training, we decided to approach the leadership of Crusade to ask if we could be placed in the same city for the next school year.

That is when we learned that could happen if we officially become an engaged couple. Neither of us felt ready for that step. In fact, we felt strongly that we should attend in January a conference in Little Rock, Arkansas. It was a Campus Crusade Conference specifically designed to help dating couples to ascertain if they were to take the step of marriage. That plan totally pleased both of us even though it meant her returning to Nashville and me to Austin. That meant more letter writing and long distant calls and getting very little done because of the longing and dreaming of what seemed to be God's future for us. Would January ever come?

The conference was at a Sheraton. I would think about 75 couples were there and it was truly a rich time. Don and Sally Meredith talked frankly and openly about their marriage, and it covered a full range of topics. We were even given some personal time with other presenters to discuss our future. Other couples were trying to discern if marriage was God's plan for them just like us. Sadly, many concluded that they were not to move ahead with a wedding but Becky and I whole heartly felt we were hearing a strong "Yes." I formally proposed to Becky, and she said yes. We celebrated by going out for dinner at Steak and Ale, following my call to her dad to get his blessing.

Then we began to set the date for the big event. It would take place July 3, 1977 and her dad agreed to perform the ceremony. He was bi-vocational Pastor at Parkview Methodist Church in Florence, Alabama.

20/20 Hindsight

"Plans fall for lack of counsel, but with many advisors they succeed." Prov. 15:22

It All Began When...

Life After the Honeymoon

My parents joined us on our honeymoon. (If you are thinking that is taking counseling just a little too far, you would be right.) Allow me to explain. The last night of our stay in a lovely chalet in Gatlinburg, Tennessee, my parents drove over from South Carolina, to accompany us in Nashville the next morning. They wanted to help load up a U-Haul trailer with Becky's belongings. We would then head on to our new assignment in California.

Yes, Becky and I were finally assigned to the same city-San Bernardino, the headquarters for Campus Crusade for Christ. Our assignment was to train the headquarters staff in evangelism and discipleship. We felt like settlers of the old west as we traveled across the country with our few belongings pulled behind Becky's yellow Nova. We were truly in for a lot of adventure in our new life together. We headed west while my parents headed east, returning to Clemson.

Our second Sunday in California was quite memorable. We planned to attend a large and thriving church in Riverside. The University of California in Riverside was to be the location where we would take our trainees and we were to establish a Campus Crusade group on that Campus. With that insight we decided to visit a Calvary Chapel at Riverside (It would later be named Harvest Chapel).

As we dressed for this Sunday service, Becky dressed in her best and I put on neat clean street clothes. That led to a disagreement. Becky expressed her displeasure at my choice of clothing. Being newly married, I quickly changed into a three-piece suit, white shirt, and tie.

The church turned out to be an hour away and we went in after the service started. It only took a quick look around the crowded congregation to see we looked quite out of place. Even Greg Laurie, when he came up to preach, was dressed in jeans, a fringed suede vest that looked quite appropriate with hair down to his shoulder. Now that Greg Laurie's story has been portrayed in the movie, "Jesus Revolution," we enjoy telling our story of that Sunday in August 1977.

It is amazing how God leads us. We did not make Calvary Chapel in Riverside our church home. The events following our visit to Calvary Chapel resulted in us selecting a small church in San Bernardino, The Free Methodist Church. We had paid a courtesy visit there our very first Sunday in town. Becky's father had a pastor friend who asked us to give his regards to David Rupert, the Free Methodist pastor. We had been kind but it was clear that we would be looking at other church options.

The visit to Calvary Chapel in Riverside was the start of that search. But what happened that next week after our visit to the Riverside Church changed everything. Becky had an appointment with a gynecologist and learned that she was going to need a hysterectomy. She had two benign tumors that needed to be removed. We called Pastor David Rupert who came over to pray with us. He also committed his small flock to stand with us when the time for the actual surgery to take place. And they were so supportive. Because of their kindness to us, we ended our search for another church. For the next seven years we attended The Free Methodist church.

We were able to purchase our first home on G street. It was built in 1935 and the couple who had lived there from the beginning had decorated it in pink and gray, Eleanor Roosevelt's favorite colors. The owners had both passed and shortly later the house was put on the market, and we purchased it. We moved in on September 13, 1977, with plans to remake it into our place.

Becky wanted to be a mother and I had not been too keen on being a dad. I was assured that my feeling about this would change after we were married for a while. This had been one of the topics we had talked over with the counselors at the Little Rock conference. We conveniently tabled that conversation. Nevertheless, we decided to get information on adoption.

We learned that in California you had to be married for four years before you would even be considered for adoption and the likelihood of adopting an infant was almost zero. We decided to put our name on the list for future adoptions.

After Becky recovered from her surgery, we busied ourselves with redecorating our home, exploring Southern California, and training the new staff assigned to us by taking them to the campus of the University of California in Riverside. Four years passed quickly. Looking back, they were such enjoyable years.

I digress to tell you one misadventure that happened. Crusade was known for contact evangelism. That meant deliberately putting yourself in situations where the possibility of sharing the gospel could occur. It was a day to set aside other activities and go to where one might be used to tell others about Jesus. All the staff were to take the challenge for the day. We would come back the next day and report what happened.

Becky and I along with three staff women we worked with, decided to drive into the Farmer's Market in Los Angeles for that very purpose. Becky and I had been there once before and loved the atmosphere where many tourists and others gathered for the fresh products sold there. We all loaded it into the yellow Nova.

On our way out of San Bernardino, we stopped at the Triple A office so Evelyn could get a map detailing our direction. I proceed to a nearby gas station to fill the tank. On the way out of the station we saw in the middle of the street a large young Hispanic woman flailing her arms and screaming, "Help me. Help me." In a parking lot on the opposite side of the road I saw a gray-haired man wildly driving around the parking lot in an old, brown vehicle. It appeared that he was intent on getting into the street and somehow targeting the woman. I had read about human slave trafficking, and that was exactly what I thought was taking place.

I pulled into the lane next to the girl and motioned for her to get into the front seat with Becky and myself. She sat next to the passenger door. By the time this had taken place the man in the old car was on my rear, flashing his headlights and blowing his horn. I began to drive furiously trying to leave him behind.

We were praying. I asked the girl where the police station was. She pointed straight ahead. Not daring to stop, I drove through red lights. The prayers from Becky and the two ladies in the backseat became more intense. But we did not lose Mr. Pursuer. And we were driving away from the city. I was becoming like a chase scene in a movie.

I asked the girl, "Who is that man?"

"He is a bad man. He is taking me to a bad place." She replied.

This confirmed my theory.

Eventually we drove into the parking lot of a large store named, "FedCo." I said out loud, "Maybe we can lose him here."

But no, he was still right behind me. Seeing that this wasn't working, I decided to head back to the city taking Mills Street heading east.

Then our "new friend" said, "I'll jump out and lose him in the store."

I reached over Becky and grabbed onto her arm with a firm "No." Then we headed back to the center of the city. By this time my compassion was running out and I said very firmly. "I want you to tell me who that man is and where is he taking you?"

He had now come up on my right when she said, "He is my parole officer, and he is taking me to jail."

I immediately stopped at a major intersection. She jumped out of my car and attempted to jump into a pickup truck. Her parole officer had also stopped and was now out of his car coming toward us. He approached her with handcuffs before she could successfully commandeer the pick-up. The truck driver sped off. I blocked her from running in the opposite direction.

By then three of us were in the center traffic. He looked at me and said, "I have you license plate number, and I am going to have you arrested."

I got back into the car and informed my passengers what had just happened. We headed back to pick up Evelyn who waited very puzzled and patiently for our return.

Once we clued her into our crazy adventure, the group encouraged me to find the police station and turn myself in.

When I explained to the dispatcher who I was and what had happened, she was totally clueless but advised me to go home and just wait until something further developed. That is what we did. The plan to proceed on to the Farmer's Market was aborted. I was too rattled anyway.

About six that evening a call came. The parole offer's name was Mr. Brown.

"I'm calling just to thank you for what you did today."

"THANK ME?"

"If you hadn't picked up my parolee, I would have never gotten her back into my car. She had jumped out of my car where you saw her. I thought you knew her, and it had been planned that you would take her from there."

"She herself told me that she didn't know you, but that you had thought you were helping her. She told me about the prayer in the car. By the way, I am a Christian too. Because of your witness, I was able to talk with her about the Lord."

Before he hung up, Mr. Brown said, "By the way, you are a good driver."

20/20 Hindsight.

We may not always hear the word from God exactly right, but if we are available and willing, He will even take our misunderstandings and turn them into good for His glory.

It All Began When...

Back to Alabama

Becky and I returned to visit our support team living in Florence, Alabama. It was the summer of 1978, a year after our wedding. In April 1977, Spiritual Counterfeits Project, out of Berkley California published their journal with the theme of Thanatology. Inside was an article about Elizabeth Kubler-Ross. She was the tiny Swiss Psychologist who was the rising high priest of the whole arena of the study of death and dying. I do not recall how the journal had come into my hands, but I read it with great interest. One of the noted insights into the work of Ms. Kubler-Ross was that she had two spirit guides she entertained named "Willie and Anka."

The reason the writers included this in their writing was that having a proclivity and an admitted involvement of this nature would tend to make the conclusions she was drawing in her research suspect.

Somehow as we drove to Florence, we learned that while we were there, Elizabeth Kubler-Ross would be speaking at Norton Auditorium on the campus of the University of North Alabama. Becky received her undergraduate degree from UNA. We decided we want to hear her lecture.

It turned out to be sponsored by a group of clergy from the community surrounding the campus and despite it being a summer night, the attendance was very good. We ended our trip to Florence by driving right to the lecture, arriving near the end of the evening. We were there in time to hear her conclusions regarding her research. Succinctly she declared that based on her research all deaths are met with wonderful positive outcomes. There are no reasons to be concerned with your own death, or the passing of someone you love. The audience sat in rapt attention. They gave her a rousing ovation.

A friend of Becky's came rushing up so happy to greet us and excited about what she had heard. She had been so worried about her dad who was quite ill and not a professing Christian. Now she was so relieved. We were so alarmed.

I made my way to talk with Ms. Ross. A crowd was around her but eventually I was able to get her attention. I inquired, "I understand you have two spirit guides."

Enthusiastically she responded, "Yes, their names are Willie and Anka. They are so wonderful." Then her mood shifted to suspicion, "How did you learn this?"

I had a copy of the journal from SCP in my pocket and I produced it for her to see.

Then her demeanor became almost hostile. She held out her hands toward the paper I produced and sharply she said, "Get that away from me." Then she abruptly turned her back on me and began engaging with others.

We then went to see a supporter of our ministry, Attorney Jeff Kellor, a fine Christian man in the community who had been a part of inviting Mrs. Kubler-Ross to speak. I told him what we had experienced, and he was very concerned.

He invited me to come to the debriefing meeting the next morning for those who had worked toward this event. He wanted them to hear what I had learned. The address was at an Episcopal church in neighboring Sheffield.

The next morning, Jess Keller introduced me to the group, and I was able to recount the experience I had had the night before. I am sure there were mostly negative reactions within the group. They had undoubtedly sacrificed their time, if not some treasure to pull this event off.

The Episcopal priest who was hosting the meeting, looking right at me said, "The Devil always has his distractors." But the consensus of the group, voiced by Mr. Keller was, "Ms. Ross will never be invited by this group again to speak in this area."

I left feeling that God had really used us.

20/20 Hindsight

Paul wrote to the Galatians, "But even if we or an angel from heaven should preach a gospel other than the one we preached to you, let them be under God's curse."

It All Began When...

U.C. Riverside

I took one of the headquarter's staff with me to the University of California at Riverside. As a trainer of new staff our job was to lead them into essential experiences they would need in the categories of evangelism and discipleship. I was always on the lookout for opportunities to engage individuals (in this case university students) in examining the claims of Christ and the gospel. UCR (University of California at River) was a small but highly academic schooling the UC system. It is one of the two land grant schools in the system. Much like Clemson.

On this day our approach was to engage an available student by having them read a brief article in a colorful magazine published by Campus Crusade. The article we choose was focused on the truth claims of Jesus, highlighting how He had fulfilled Old Testament prophesies.

What qualified a student as being available in our mind was that they were alone and in a relaxed situation. We had prayed prior to getting to the UCR campus that God would prepare a student to be willing to talk with us, hear the gospel and be receptive to the message of salvation. Of course, we prayed we would be tactful and directed to this person.

It wasn't long after walking on the grounds that our footsteps were led to a young man lounging on the lawn in the warm California sun. Following a brief introduction, we asked him if he would be willing to read the article and share his opinion of the content with us. In the introduction we observed that he was of an Asian dissent. His name was Wes, but the last name was not a typically Asian name and he was a grad student studying Soil Science. Wes was willing to read the article, so we waited respectfully as he read. We both were praying silently that the Lord would speak to him.

Shortly, he completed the reading and gave his opinion on the article. His overall response was positive. He revealed that his mother was Buddhist, and his father was Lutheran but essentially, he was not raised in a religious home. However, he was open to learning more about the Christian faith.

The academic year was winding down, so I suggested that I bring him a copy of More than a Carpenter by Josh McDowell. He could read it over the summer break and then we would get back in the fall to talk further. He agreed. All summer I prayed for Wes Gestring.

When September came, I contacted Wes and invited him to a little small group Bible study I was starting with several other guys who were also exploring Christianity. Wes joined in.

Another opportunity to connect emerged when a larger group of students decided to go to Magic Mountain, an amusement park in Valencia. By his own admission, that was a turning point spiritually for Wes. He met other UCR students who were believers and after that he began to take Jesus seriously.

In his remaining two semesters prior to getting his master's degree, Wes became very hungry to grow and availed himself regularly of opportunities to study and fellowship despite the pressures on him to complete his graduate research. He completed his thesis in June 1979. And I was completely honored when he dedicated it to me.

Upon graduation he went on to complete his studies of Agronomy at Colorado State University, accomplishing his Doctorate in 1982. But the story of Wes and me continues years later. You will want to read his own words in the last section of this book entitled, "The Rest of the Story."

20/20 Hindsight

The gospel is appealing but it has its greatest appeal when it is fleshed out in the lives of those whose lives have been changed by believing in Jesus.

It All Began When...

Ursula

Ursula (not her real name but she looked like the Ursula on "Disney's The Little Mermaid") sat across our dining room table from Becky and me. Ursula was a social worker from the county's department of social services. She had come to begin our adoption process. With her husky voice she informed us that if we told her we were born again Christians she would not be able to place a child in our home. We looked at each other and I proceeded to tell her that we were indeed born-again Christians.

With that startling and awkward introduction, she proceeded to explain that in California the birth mother's only legal right was to dictate the religious preference of her child's upbringing. If she preferred her child be raised Buddhist, the adopting parents would either need to be Buddhist or commit to raising the child as a Buddhist. Then she went on to tell us that a young woman in the county was pregnant and she wanted her baby to be in the home of someone from Campus Crusade for Christ. What had started out as a huge negative suddenly turned very positive.

If we were to receive this child, we would need to accelerate our process of applying to adopt. We readily agreed to begin the required group sessions and the accompanying homework immediately. There were six sessions and pages and pages of questions and an autobiography that we had to complete. In addition, we began to arrange our home for the coming infant. As we engaged in this process, Ursula seemed increasingly pleased with us as perspective parents.

Time passed when the baby we were desiring should have been born and subsequently placed in our home. We had heard nothing about the mother's progress with the birth. I eventually put a call into Ursula inquiring about why we had not heard anything.

She matter-of-factly said, "Did I not tell you? The mother changed her mind."

That was more jolting than learning she would not place a child in our home if we were born again Christians. "But you are approved to adopt so we will be talking about you having another child. I feel you two are strong enough parents to take a teenager. Would you be open to a teenager?"

I hope I didn't sound anywhere as angry as I felt when I said. "NO."

A few weeks later Ursula was again across the dining room table from us to ask if we would be interested in twin boys, four years old. They were not yet cleared for adoption, but we could take them as fosdops (Children placed as foster children readying for legal adoption). My dad had been a twin and I was told that alternating generations were probable for conceiving twins. That idea appealed to me. And Becky went along it with as well.

We were first to meet these boys at a Halloween party for potential adopting parents to meet prospective adoptable children. The children wore costumes. When we got to the party, neither of the twins were there. This was another disappointment.

We learned the next week that a psychiatrist who had assessed the boys had concluded that they were not to be placed together in a home. They came from a family of 9 children and both parents were incarcerated. The mother was in prison for child abuse. She had abused one of the twins physically. Consequently, their exposure to abuse had made them abusive to each other.

"Would you be interested in one of the boys?" we were asked.

Despite our disappointment we said, "Yes."

On December 5, 1980, Joseph Bradley, a vivacious four-year-old came to our home.

Almost the first thing, he asked me, "Do you like bad boys?"

I was certainly taken off guard, but I replied "Yes, I like all boys. And I don't believe you are a bad boy."

Later the social worker who brought him to our home highly complemented my answer.

Bradley seemed highly intent on testing us on that answer and because of his prior abuse we were not ever to administer corporal punishment for his out-of-control behavior.

One of those behaviors was biting, particularly biting Becky. She would call the social worker to determine what to do. The advice was to have him bite a teddy bear, a wet washcloth or perhaps an onion. Nothing worked. Then one day after he bit her particularly hard, Becky calmly and deliberately bit him back. She left on his arm a distinct red mark. He expressed shock and anguish with tears. Then Becky called the social worker to inform her.

She said, "I hate to hear that, but let's see if that works."

It did. He never bit Becky again.

But there were fun and funny moments as well. He came with a full set of street vocabulary. One morning he joined me in the bathroom as I got out of the shower. He proceeded to name body parts by the street terms, and I corrected him with the correct words, at least the ones we practiced in our home. Instead of "ass," his new family says, "bottom" etc.

Later Becky took Bradley to Loma Linda University Hospital for a doctor's visit. As they were descending the building in a crowded elevator, Bradley stood facing the back of the man standing in front of him. In the quiet of the elevator, Bradley reached up and patted the man's rears and said loudly, "Bottom." The man turned to see who touched him and Bradley reached up, touching his front, and said, "Penis."

Becky said there were muted snickers from the crowd. The man turned beet red and the door opened for the first floor. The people got off releasing their hushed laughs. Becky pulled Bradley aside and affirmed him for using the right words but instructed him that those words should only be used in privacy not when a lot of people can hear them. That seemed to have worked.

But not all lessons were taken so quickly. Bradley's anger outbursts were not so easily squelched. When we would get him together with his brother, it would not be long until they were poking and pelting each other until there were tears. When that happened, we were so grateful that they were not put together in our home.

20/20 Hindsight

God works through very flawed people to accomplish his plans for our lives.

It All Began When...

A Life Changing Letter

A letter from the International Graduate School of Theology (or ISOT) arrived at our home. It informed me that with my studies at the Institute of Biblical Studies that I had completed along with my years of service with Campus Crusade for Christ I had accumulated 50% of the credits I needed to complete a master's in divinity. What I needed to do to complete the other 50% and receive the degree was to become a full-time student at ISOT, complete two internships: one domestic and one international.

ISOT classes were conducted in a portion of the headquarters of Campus Crusade where we served in the training Center. It was an easy drive from our house. Oddly I was intrigued by the possibility. I had no aspirations to receive a degree since I was enjoying my work in the training center. I had not long before moved into the role of director. Besides, now I was a parent to a five-year-old that was proving to be quite a handful. Traveling internationally to fulfill the requirements of the international internship seemed impossible and the domestic internship sounded very unappealing. I had no aspirations to work in a local church. The idea of being a pastor was repulsive.

I set the letter aside and tried to forget about it. But I couldn't let it go. The notion of leaving a project half completed genuinely bothered me. It seems like such a waste. And the fact that the location of the school was so convenient just wouldn't let me push it aside. The more I considered the proposition the more the completing of the rest of the school's requirements seemed like a challenge I just had to face. That challenge included studying both Greek and Hebrew. That certainly wasn't something I relished.

An additional objection that came through in a daunting question was, Would our team of supporters join me financially in this adventure? They had proven over the years to be so faithful and generous. I could believe this team would give if I was discipling many for Christ, but to put something of a pause on that activity, and go to classes? Would they remain motivated to support me and my family?

There was a deadline to respond to this letter. It fell after the end of the Christmas season. That Christmas we had planned to spend Thanksgiving in Florence with Becky's folks and Christmas with mine in Clemson. Most of our support team lived in and around those communities. This would provide a time to talk face to face with those who had been giving to our ministry. We would explain the possible changes in our focus and ask them how they felt about continuing to support us.

We took a red eye special from LAX to Birmingham with a lengthy lay-over in Dallas. Naturally we had not slept before boarding in California. Three tired travelers found a convenient spot close to the departure gate to wait out the 3 hours for the flight. About 15 minutes after our departure time, I woke up in a panic. Rushing to the attendant at the gate I breathlessly asked about the status of our flight.

She said, "That flight has left." As my heart sank, she turned and looked out the window at the runway. Then she said, "I can't believe it! It is still on the tarmac!" She promptly got on the phone and called out to the pilot.

I couldn't hear what she was saying but I was right in assuming she was telling pilot he had left 3 passengers behind. The plane was making its way back to the gate and we sheepishly got on. I felt so bad that we had made those travelers late for their holiday destinations.

As we walked through first class a gentleman leaned over and looking straight at me said, "You owe it to me that this plane came back for you."

"Oh, how is that?" I asked.

"My luggage was lying on the ground, and I refused to let us take off until they got it on board. For the longest time they just couldn't seem to see my luggage."

I said, "Sir, I think my angels kept hiding it from them."

God takes care of us despite my own lack of diligence.

I don't know how that happened, but I do believe that God was intervening on our behalf to get us to that important trip back to family and friends. And as I shared with them the thoughts regarding what we were considering, I found receptive and affirming hearts. We returned to California knowing our lives were decidedly going to take on a new direction.

20/20 Hindsight

"The one who calls you is faithful, and he will do it." I Thessalonians 5:24

It All Began When...

England

We boarded a plane again at LAX. It was June 1983, and the three of us were flying again this time to London. I could hardly believe it. I was off to complete my International Internship. It was one of the hurdles I expected the hardest to accomplish and it came together so rapidly and perfectly.

The small Free Methodist Church we attended became a source for this next adventure. We learned that a pastor of a Free Methodist Church in Frodsham, England was seeking to spend the summer studying at Fuller Theological Seminary. He was offering his home and car for the summer provided the one sent to England would pastor his church in his absence. That was the ideal goal of an international ministry experience. We could speak the language and we could offer our home for Rev. Ball to use. A clear bonus was Becky's excitement about a summer in Britain.

Richard Scott was an attorney in our San Bernardino church. He was such a good friend. He had introduced me to the game of racquetball (and consistently beat me every time). Plus, he had taken care of the legal documentation for our adoption of Bradley. When he learned about our travels to England, he came forth with the funds for our travels there and back. We were on our way!!

Skip Ball met us in London to ride the train with us back to Frodsham. It would be the only briefing I would get on the summer work. I listened intently as he told me about the history of the church and the spiritual state of the congregation, mostly new believers.

There was the one new believer who was recovering from addiction to alcohol and because of his struggle, no one in the church was even to visit a pub "to help keep him from stumbling." (As you may know, pubs were the community's fast food in the tiny towns of England). That proved to be quite a sacrifice for the fellow members.

One person I was to be aware of was Mr. Dyson. He was recently widowed and rather new to the church.

I also learned that while we were there that summer Billy Graham was leading a crusade and would be preaching several nights at Anfield in nearby Liverpool. The church was joining in, and I had been assigned to receive training in supervising the counselors from the area. That was certainly in line with my work with Campus Crusade.

There were a lot of adjustments, and many were surprising in the category of language. The first Sunday I met Mr. Dyson. I expected an elderly man, stooped and gray, instead he was a youthful looking middle ager, but very proper. I mentioned to him that I would like, while there that Sunday, to have lunch with him. He seemed to appreciate that.

With all the business of adjusting to the business of my new role, I had to always remember to wear a clerical collar. Skip insisted that whenever I was in public that was the proper look for an American clergy. Otherwise, they would believe I was with a cult. The time with Mr. Dyson got shoved aside. Additionally, since we were prohibited from lunching in one of the nearby pubs, this proved problematic. But eventually

I discovered in Frodsham a small place to have lunch called the Patisserie.

With that discovery, I asked Mr. Dyson after church on Sunday if we might have lunch together that week. He seemed a bit startled but agreed, telling me he would give me a ring that afternoon to confirm arrangements.

A family had invited us over for lunch following the Sunday service. Andrew was the father of the family, and he was so accommodating. He was the one who had taught me this little ditty:

"I eats me peas with honey,
I've done it all me life.
It makes the peas taste funny,
But it keeps them on me knife."

Presently at the table I mentioned to Andrew Mr. Dyson's strange reaction to my request to have lunch. Andrew knowingly responded, "Do you know what he thought you were saying?"

"Well, I assumed he knew I wanted to take him to lunch at the Patisserie."

Andrew shook his head, "We really don't do that sort of thing here. He thinks you were asking to come to his house for a meal."

I was mortified. It was shortly after that that Mr. Dyson rang. "I have it all arranged. My daughter will prepare the meal."

"Oh Mr. Dyson, that was not at all what I had in mind." I explained my misunderstanding.

But he insisted. So, Becky, Bradley and I made our way to his home that Wednesday and had a lovely visit and meal with him and his daughter.

20/20 Hindsight

I am in good company inviting myself to lunch. Didn't Jesus invite Himself to Zacchaeus' house for a meal?

It All Began When...

A Baby Girl

It was prior to our trip to England when our social worker came by our house for a visit. We were packing for our trip. It was such a contrast to her first visit with us two years earlier when she told us about not placing a child with us if we were born again Christians.

She was in a very relaxed and upbeat mood. She came to tell us that the Department of Social Services had a baby girl who was to be born in August. If we were interested, she could be ours. We of course told her of our pending trip to England just days away and that we would not be back when the baby was due. She assured us that that would not be a problem. The child would, like Bradley, be a fosdop and would be kept for a while in a foster care home for newborns. The earliest we could receive her would be November.

She informed us, based on the birth mother's current dire situation, that we would need to agree to take this child in for visits with the mother. She would be put on a plan to turn her life around and could possibly get her baby back. We had no objection to those terms.

Before Ursula left our house that day, she made a most revealing comment to us.

She simply stated, "I have so admired the faith you have. I wish I could have it too."

We were pleasantly surprised at such an admission. I asked her, "If I gave you a book, <u>More than a Carpenter,</u> would you read it?"

I explained that it was a short book written by Josh McDowell. We knew the author personally and she would find it easy to read. She said she would.

On our way to the airport, I had dropped the copy of the book off by her office. She was not there. And the rest of the summer, we continued to pray for her. Our hearts grew so heavy for her, and we so looked forward to seeing her again.

When we returned to San Bernardino, we put in a call to social services to let them know we were back. When a week or so passed, memories of what happened the first time when promises of an infant to us left us wondering if there was a repeat of that experience in the making. But eventually a social worker from the department called to inform us that we were assigned a case worker and she wanted to come by to talk with us about receiving the baby who had been born August 6. She scheduled a visit to our home.

She was a very pleasant and professional woman who assured us that the baby we hoped for was healthy and living with a foster mom who specialized in newborn infants. We were able to schedule a visit to see the little girl, but there were procedures that we had to accomplish before she would be coming to our home. We were elated.

In that visit with our new social worker, I eventually asked her about Ursula. I could tell she was extremely reluctant to tell us anything. Then I told her about giving Ursula the book and I wanted to follow up with her about it. Once she understood my motive, she dropped a bombshell.

"Oh, she is no longer with the agency."

I pushed further, "Could you please get a contact from her? I gave her a book before we left for England. I would like to get it back and talk with her about it."

Then our new social worker confided in us, "She was living with me as she struggled all summer with depression. And eventually was so overcome that she took her own life. But she talked about the two of you often and she read and reread the book you gave her."

Our joy over being able to see our future child was inundated with this news about a woman we had learned to love deeply.

20/20 Hindsight

To love and love deeply is a costly proposition.

It All Began When...

Spiritual Warfare

The precious little girl we had met one time at Bonnie Miracle's home (that was really the foster mom's name) was brought to us in a basket by Joyce, one of the social workers with the agency. It was November 5, 1984. For a while she was permitted to sleep in the room with Becky and me, but we were told we would need to move into a house that provided her with her own room. I certainly was willing, but that seemed like such a tall order. How could we afford that? We had a year to figure it out.

During this year I was busy with Greek, Hebrew, and hermeneutics. It was demanding. I was now beginning to consider where my domestic internship would be. The thought of serving in a church was becoming more exciting to me, based on the experience in Frodsham. I loved being a pastor in a local church.

My church heritage was in the Wesleyan Church. Pastor Derric Johnson, who I attribute my turning to Christ back in 1969, had come from Skyline Wesleyan outside of San Diego. He has long since moved on and I had failed to maintain contact with him anyway. Skyline was under the leadership of John Maxwell. I only knew about him. But I felt so impressed to write Skyline and asked if they would permit me to serve there during the next summer. The letter went out and I waited.

One of the classes I took in Seminary was taught by R.C. Sproul. He was with us as a visiting professor for a week. His topic was cults. An assignment that came with the class was to research cults that he had not covered during the week he taught us. On the list of possible choices was Nichiren Shochu Buddhism. It instantly caught my attention because I had begun a phone discipleship with a women named Helen in Los Angeles who was converted to Christ out of Nichiren Shochu. We met on the phone every Sunday evening and I was helping her get grounded in Christianity. (She was led to Christ through the influence of a mutual friend, Eric Show who was a pitcher for the San Diego Padres).

I knew nothing about her Buddhist beliefs, but I learned that she was more than willing to expose me to the cult she had followed. That was a win-win for her and for me. I traveled to Los Angeles to attend a meeting in a home where the participants sat on the floor in front of a small statue called a Dai-Gohonzon. It was a replica of an original and much larger one at the base of Mt. Fuji in Japan.

They chanted to the Dai-Gohonzon. It was a very specific chant that I learned from testimonials resulted in positive life changes to those who chose to engage in this "worship." "These witnesses" were set free from addictions, received financial benefits, promotions in their job, or even experienced physical healing. It reminded me in some ways of an evangelistic service. Helen said if I wish to learn more, the regional temple for this sect was in Rancho Cucamonga. She said I may wish to visit it as well, but I felt from her input I had sufficient information to write the brief report the class required of me.

While seminary certainly preoccupied me, Becky was dealing with the various requirements coming our way from the social worker. I had joined her for a visit to Elizabeth's birth mom but when the second visit came around, I had a major conflict and could not go.

I was eager to hear what had happened that evening. I learned that the mother had taken the baby in her arms as Becky sat and watched. Then she began to say foreign words over the infant. I asked Becky if it might be that she was speaking in tongues?

She replied, "I don't think so, it sounded more like a chant." Then she said she would like to take the baby to church with her.

"Did you find out where the church is located?"

"Rancho Cucamonga."

"I wonder if she is a Nicherin Shochu Buddhist?" I speculated.

We placed a call to our social worker and told her what had happened during the visit that afternoon.

She was a feisty woman who promptly said, "I will call her and find out."

A few minutes later she called back and confirmed that indeed our daughter's birth mother was in this cult. We knew immediately that our battle was very much a spiritual one. We began to pray and had our church pray as well that God would confuse the spirits that were at play in Elizabeth's future.

At first the mother began to improve, enabling her to check off the list of requirements for retaining the baby. But about two months later, much to everyone's surprise, she simply disavowed that the baby was hers. Which meant Elizabeth was free to be fully adopted by us.

That Sunday we announced the good news to our praying church family. We held our baby in our arms before the congregation. Following the announcement, we placed her back in the nursery for the duration of the service. As soon as the service concluded we went back to retrieve her, only to be informed that after we had left her sitting on a baby seat placed on the floor, a metal easel suddenly toppled over barely missing hitting the baby on the head.

The lady who was attending to her was very distraught. She told us, "The windows were all closed. No one was around her. There was no wind. There was no apparent earthquake. The easel toppled over, totally unprovoked, but Elizabeth was untouched."

That evening, I shared the incident with Helen in Los Angeles. She calmly took it in. Then told me that the night when she gave her life to Jesus, she was at a friend's house in San Diego. She knelt by the bed in their quest room. When she had finished praying, before she could stand up, two large stereo speakers mounted on the wall above the bed suddenly broke loose and toppled down barely missing her head.

20/20 Hindsight

We truly do wrestle against principalities and forces in heavenly places. And our enemy is intent on lying, stealing, and killing. But our God is greater.

It All Began When…

Skyline Singles

I received a letter from Chuck Shores, single adult pastor at Skyline Wesleyan Church inviting me to come for the summer to serve alongside of him in his work with singles. This began the phase in my seminary study where I experienced service in a local church, state side. Not just any local church but Skyline, a church of 3000 just out of beautiful San Diego.

Chuck worked diligently finding housing for a first portion of the summer near the church and through my contacts with Campus Crusade we were able to house sit a home where the family left for the last part of the summer, it was in far north San Diego County. We packed what we could and began a truly great adventure.

On our first Sunday we attended the Single's gathering numbering about 80 singles ranging in age of late 20's to those in retirement. They were most welcoming and energetic, just like their leader. Chuck had come into the pastorate for Singles, having been a plumber. He was truly a pied piper to the congregation he shepherded.

The next Monday I reported to Chuck's office. I commented quite naively, "It is amazing to me that many adults in this church have never been married."

"You think they have never been married?" he queried.

"How can they be active in a Christian church if they are divorced?" Unwittingly, I revealed a bias that had been passed on to me in my upbringing in a very conservative church. Divorce was essentially equivalent of the unpardonable sin.

With that conversation, Chuck began to pull from his library, books on divorce and remarriage. It was an impressive stack. He also gave me a cassette player and some tapes. And my first assignment was to spend the day in the office alone reading, studying, and praying. I was to ask God to speak to me.

I chaffed at the assignment but dutifully began exploring the material put before me, but it was an assignment I really had no choice but to fulfill. I perused over the options and eventually landed on listening to a set of tapes about divorce and remarriage given by Chuck himself. (I didn't realize it at the time, but I know now I'm an auditory learner). By listening to Chuck's teaching on tape, I figured it would help me understand better the man I was to learn from for the next two months.

The essence of what I learned that day was the scriptural teaching on divorce and remarriage taken from I Corinthians 7:10-16. In short, Paul was advocating marriage, but not staying in a marriage at the expense of diluting one's commitment to Jesus. A marriage that brought compromise with a deep walk with the Lord is to end.

Undergirding this clear teaching was deep compassion on the part of the presenter (Chuck) for those who must be willing to forgo a marriage and open the door for divorce. I found myself alone in this office confessing to God how wrong my self-righteous attitude had been to the few individuals whom I had known that had gone through divorce.

The primary one was my sister. When she was still a teenager, she entered a marriage with another teenager. While

I was enjoying college and my early stages of spiritual growth they had married, and I felt some indignation that she did this way too young. And then when I was "out saving the world" she and this young man ended in divorce. I had no toleration for her choices. It was a good thing I was not around while it was happening. All she would have gotten from me was condemnation. Unfortunately, I expressed it to her in a letter.

Now, here I was confronted with my own lack of compassion and unwillingness to approach her with any possibility of forgiveness. Her situation was not the only one I regretted over that afternoon. There were others whose names I could not even recall that incurred my disdain. Fortunately, with my sister, I was able to seek her forgiveness through a carefully written letter of apology.

My heart was broken and mended that day, and I was able to process that with Chuck when he came back to see how the day had gone. He never stated it overtly, but I could tell he was quite pleased with what had been accomplished on my first day on the job. It was only shortly afterwards that he announced to the congregation of single adults that one of my assignments for the summer was to organize a divorce recovery ministry. His announcement was the first time I had heard that assignment.

Much to my surprise and even my pleasure, along with a group of divorced singles, a divorce recovery ministry was organized and served that community for several years.

Yes, what had been a summer internship turned into 7 years. Here is how that happened. A stir within the singles congregation began to happen for me to move from San Bernardino to San Diego and join in serving the group. The idea of serving Skyline Singles and serving under the pastorship of John Maxwell appealed to me immensely but there were some enormous obstacles. First, I was to finish my degree at the International Graduate School of Theology in San Bernardino. The answer to that problem was to switch to a seminary there in San Diego; Bethel-west.

That seemed minor to the next issue. To live in San Diego was considerably more expensive than remaining in San Bernardino. We were buying a house, a house too small for our family. Social services had already decreed that we needed to move. More money was certainly going to be needed. How was that going to happen?

On the following Sunday night, Chuck asked me to stay home and rest. He complemented me on the hard work and encouraged us to take that Sunday evening when the Singles meet and just take a break. It felt something like that day I was isolating myself in the office. I chaffed at the assignment but did as I was told.

The next time the Single adult class met, Chuck had me come to the front of the gathering. After lauding me with compliments, he announced that the group, when they met without me, committed to making up the financial gap I needed in order to make the move to come to Skyline so that we could continue the ministry that had begun that summer. Becky and I were overwhelmed and how could we do anything else but take the many steps of making the transition.

By the time the fall semester started at Bethel-west I had transitioned. We were in the house now suitable for Elizabeth to have her own room. My credits at ISOT transferred and I was now taking classes on the campus not far from where we lived. And we were so enjoying being in a church that was pastored by one of the greatest leaders in the country.

A year later Chuck announced his resignation to take his own church. I still had not completed my master's in divinity.

What was going to happen to me? That question was soon answered when John Maxwell asked me to take the position vacated by Chuck for the next year. It was a trial to see if I was truly ready for this leadership role. The church would compensate me on expenses but since I had not yet completed my degree or been ordained, I was to continue my financial support in the current manner. I agreed.

Even though I was diligently working on finishing the degree, studying for ordination, leading the singles (including carrying on the divorce recovery meetings) and doing my best to be a husband and father, it was an amazing year of growth and accomplishment.

The next year I was ordained, legally the father to Elizabeth, and John expressed his pleasure at the work that I had done to the degree that they officially hired me on as the Single Adult Minister of Skyline Wesleyan.

Oh, I failed to mention that our house in San Bernardino had sold, so our next adventure was to buy a home in San Diego.

20/20 Hindsight

Don't tell me that faith the size of a mustard seed, when it is placed in a great and good God, can't move a mountain.

It All Began When…

A Flat Time

We bought a new Dodge Caravan. Our Citation was proving too small for our family, and it was showing signs of aging so along with the financial help of my parents, we bought for the first time in our marriage a brand-new car.

We only had the Caravan for a few months when we had an occasion to take it from East San Diego County to Mission Valley, the entertainment/tourist center of the county. The event was the premier of a movie that was locally produced. The script had been written by one of the women in our Single's ministry, Kathy Harris. We were excited to attend such a momentous evening.

We had gotten a bit of a late start (which was par for the four of us). We had only progressed about 5 miles when a tire went flat on our new vehicle. Of course, I had not bothered to read the owner's manual. I had changed a flat tire before but never in a car that had the tire mounted underneath the automobile. I didn't even know where the jack was kept. That certainly impeded our progress.

I lay underneath the Caravan hitting the suspended spare with a rock, but that proved futile. Where was the jack? In my desperation, I spotted close by on the freeway an emergency phone. As I was making my way to the phone to call for help, a car pulled up and two men got out and asked if they could help. Naturally, I was delighted with the help.

They knew exactly what to do. They showed me the jack mounted under the hood. I would have never guessed that. Then they proceeded to detach the spare from below the rear. With their skill it came off easily and together that had us ready to roll again. GOD ANSWERS PRAYER, and I highly suspect it was Becky, sitting patiently in the car with two impatient kids, whose prayers were answered.

I offered to pay the two men and they absolutely refused.

Then they told me their side of the story. They were a father and son duo. They had passed us as they headed west on the freeway when they spotted our situation. What they noted was a pair of legs sticking out from under the car and on the legs were a pair of white shoes. They immediately believed it was a woman in distress, so they took the next exit and came back. By the time they reached us, I was no longer under the car but headed to the phone. But, despite me not being a damsel in distress, they stopped anyway. It was a good laugh, but I never wore those white shoes again.

We made it to the premier, which was a good thing, because as far as I know that movie received such bad reviews, it was never shown again.

2020 Hindsight

Hebrews 1:14 asked the question, "Are not all angels ministering spirits sent to serve those who will inherit salvation?" The answer is yes and sometimes they come disguised as a black man with his adult son.

It All Began When…

Noni

A woman who had been attending the Singles came to me and asked if she could have an appointment to meet me in my office during the week. That was not at all unusual. I did a high amount of personal counseling. I had been assigned early on to conduct all the pre-marriage counseling in the church. That for the most part was fun. Becky joined me in that endeavor. We did a joint session on sexual adjustment in marriage in a group setting. She taught the women, and I taught the men. I teased her that she was the "Dr. Ruth of Skyline."

Then, because so many of the singles were divorced, I had many sad opportunities to sit with them as they continued to grieve the losses. We even began a grief recovery ministry for those who lost a mate by death. Those were deep painful times of joining with those going through their losses.

The woman asking for the appointment was named Noni. I had seen Noni in the congregation. She was a lady who presented herself well. I didn't get the impression that we would be talking about divorce or the death of a mate. I felt it would be something unique and it was. When we met that day, I learned that she had grown up in the home of a pastor but had rebelled. She married a successful businessman, and they had one son. After they divorced some years after their son's birth, she too had become a successful businesswoman in her own right. But despite her accomplishments she had developed a strong hunger for God. That hunger had drawn her to Skyline and to the Singles.

As I continued to explore her history, especially her spiritual history, I discovered that she lacked a personal commitment to Jesus. I was able to lead her to open her heart to the Lord and trust Him as her Lord and Savior. She was powerfully broken, and her transformation was amazing.

There were painful and dark things she told me concerning her past. She had become deeply embroiled in the New Age Movement. She asked me if she could bring me the books, tapes, and Tarot cards she had collected. Of course, I agreed. She told me it would be bags and bags of stuff. The thought came to me from the book of Acts (18-19). At Ephesus, those who had been into the occult practices brought their paraphernalia together and they discarded them in a large fire. I asked her to think about us doing that with her dubious collection. She reluctantly agreed provided her identity would be protected.

A time and date were set. Our singles congregation gathered around the bon fire that was set and we sang and worshiped together rejoicing over the life that was set free. And of course, her identity was never divulged.

Later Noni came to me and confessed to an abortion she had years prior. That resulted in her participating in an abortion recovery ministry being conducted in the community by a Christian pregnancy center. She then asked if she could be trained to conduct this same ministry as an extension of our Single's group. It was called "Mended Hearts." She organized the ministry and conducted it. My role at the end of each weekend was to come and have a service that those who had suffered from abortion could have a memorial service to the child they had lost. It was always such a moving experience.

Mended Hearts lasted for 15 years. That meant years after I left Skyline Noni continued to touch the lives of women and men who had suffered through abortion.

20/20 Hindsight

God is so able to take our brokenness and bring blessing.

It All Began When…

Mostly Becky's Story

It was a Wednesday in late October 1985 at our Single Adult service. Becky was joined by a pretty young woman with long hair. She had never seen her before. As it turns out it was her first time attending, nor did she ever come back again. She was certainly of some ethnic descent and obviously pregnant. Before the meeting began Becky introduced herself and learned this young woman had 2 small children. As they chatted, Becky told her about our two adopted children and other information about our lives. The woman's neighbor had brought her to church that night but that was about as much Becky learned about her before the meeting began.

At the conclusion of the meeting the mother turned to her and asked, "When my baby is born, would you want to adopt it?" Naturally, Becky was surprised. She had been praying for our friends Andy and Teri who had been wanting to adopt a baby. They lived in Texas. She told this young lady about the couple she knew might be very interested in this woman's unborn baby. She readily gave her phone number to Becky; in turn Becky contacted our friends who were willing to pursue this possibility further. Time was of the essence since the child was due at the turn of the year.

In the meantime, Becky became very involved in getting this young mother to doctor's appointments, shopping and basically befriending her. This led to an invitation to be in the delivery room when the baby was born. Since a new year was looming, Teri and Andy were taking deliberate steps toward adoption.

Becky and I got home late and were dogged tired as we went to bed about midnight. We agreed that we hoped that this would not be the night when the mother wanting Terri and Andy to adopt her baby would go into labor. We had not gotten the words out of our mouth more than the phone rang with her on the line. Recognizing her voice I blurted out "Are you pregnant?" She calmly replied, "I've been pregnant for 9 months and I'm at the hospital about to deliver."

Now Terri and Andy pick up the story...,

Teri and I had talked off and on about possibly having a child together shortly after being married in November of 1983. In the summer of 1985, after almost two years of being married, Teri and I began to talk about taking steps to either have a child or adopt one. Teri already had three children from a previous marriage but really wanted us to have one together. However, Teri's ability to have children was severely restricted since she had had her fallopian tubes "tied" following the birth of her third child. After talking to several doctors, we determined that surgeries intended to repair such a tubal ligation seemed too risky and could not at all guarantee that she would conceive. So we explored other options and began looking at various adoption agencies in the Dallas area.

Later that summer I had the occasion to be assigned two weeks of active duty in San Diego as part of my required U. S. Marine Corps Reserve service. I attended a course of training at the Coronado Naval Air Station. Since this was during summer vacation for my stepchildren, they and Teri all flew out to San Diego to join me. During the trip we were able to visit several scenic places around San Diego. Also, since Becky and Larry had moved to the San Diego area after I had moved to Dallas, we planned for Teri and the kids to meet them and do some fun things together while I was in Coronado doing my USMCR duties.

It turns out that Larry and Becky's move to San Diego was another in a list of many occurrences that we later realized could not have been anything other than a "God thing." They had been living in San Bernardino, CA for several years while working on staff with Campus Crusade for Christ. They had gone to San Diego to as temporary interns, working with a singles ministry at their church. However, they were asked to stay on there permanently and moved from San Bernardino, just before I was slated to be out there.

During our visits with Larry and Becky, we told them about our desire to have another child and that we wanted to adopt a newborn baby if at all possible. We had no inkling how important that casual conversation was to be, nor the totally surprising way God would work in our lives as a result.

Later that fall we continued to learn about the various processes involved in traditional agency adoptions. Typically, these involved the family going through a home study and training to become certified to foster/adopt. After that the family would wait for the agency or CPS to contact them about being considered as a candidate for a particular adoption "match" Most of these children were ones who had been removed from their birth parents, abandoned, or processed through Texas Child Protective Services (CPS) for one reason or another. Several of those agencies told us that, as Teri already had three children, we would not be viewed as priority candidates for a newborn.

We also discovered something called "open" adoptions. These agencies generally had birthparents who had approached them voluntarily to see about giving up their child for various reasons. The appeal of the open adoptions to birth parents was a promise that the adoptive parents would allow some kind of future contact to be maintained with the child and the birth parents. Since traditional adoptions generally "sealed" the records of where children were placed, the open adoption approach encouraged pregnant women who were in dire circumstances to view adoption as a more favorable option for them because they would not lose contact with their child forever just because the child was adopted.

Near the end of October Teri and I made plans to visit one of these "open" agencies in Midland, TX on November 1st. The night before that interview we received a call out of the blue from Becky White. She told us that she had been burdened to pray for us to get a baby after we had visited there in the summer. Just a few days before her call to us, Becky had been approached by a young woman visiting the singles ministry. She was a single nineteen-year-old mother with two young children aged 2 and 1 year old and obviously pregnant with another child on the way. Child Protective services (CPS) had already removed these children due to her drinking and drug issues. She said that she wanted to be the one to find a home for her unborn child rather than have CPS take the child. Becky befriended her and told her about her own challenges trying to parent two adopted children. As the young mother became more comfortable talking to Becky she asked if Becky knew anyone who might want to adopt her yet unborn child. Hence the call to us on October 31, 1985.

As was later explained to us, the young mother was unable to care for another child and desperate to find someone who she could trust to give her unborn child a safe, loving home.

Becky and Larry asked us on that call, "Are you still interested?" Of course, we were just overjoyed and completely surprised and said, "You bet we are!" We learned within a few days, after Becky took the mom to some doctor appointment, that the baby was due about the first week in January.

The next day we went ahead and made our trip to Midland and had a good visit with a relatively new adoption agency that seemed very sympathetic to our circumstances and desire to adopt an infant. Then, for about the next month, after the call from Becky and Larry, we went on with life as normal without hearing much more. So, we really began wonder and prayed for God's guidance for our situation. We began to correspond more with Becky and Larry to learn more about the single mother situation. Because we had learned that the preborn baby's mother was dealing with some level of substance abuse we grew concerned that this factor could play a role in determining the health and even the viability of the unborn child. The more we learned the more concerned we became. And we wondered whether we could commit to being adoptive parents of a child that might be born with all kinds of health issues. So, we went back to God and prayed that he would give us wisdom in the matter.

Over the next month Teri and I felt like we were moving on to what we later referred to as the "wild toad's ride" in reference to the name of what had once been a roller coaster ride at Disneyland. We knew almost nothing about how a private (not through an agency) adoption worked. We asked a church friend who was an attorney if he knew someone who did interstate adoptions. Based on his recommendation we contacted and made an appointment with the attorney. Meanwhile, Teri was researching adoptions and learned that there was an organization within the Department of Human Services called the Interstate Compact Office. It had to approve any interstate transportation of a child that is to be adopted. We learned that this required reciprocal agreements between states and that both Texas and California were signatories to the Interstate Compact.

Teri also learned that an adoptive home study was required. Not only that, but the state of Texas would also only approve a home study completed by someone with at least a year of home study experience who was on their approved list. When we started asking around, we also learned that most of the people who are approved for home studies worked exclusively for adoption agencies. These social workers were not permitted to freelance and work private adoptions. This seemed like a big problem, but we soon saw another example of God's providence.

In over thirty years of being a preschool teacher, 1985 was the only year Teri ever had a social worker as a parent. Teri approached this parent and asked if she knew of anyone who might do home study for us. This parent was not certified for home studies but said that she knew a man who had been a social worker in the past but who was now a licensed counselor. She recommended that Teri call him.

Teri did call him, and he told her that, as it so happened, his counseling practice usually experienced sort of a "slow season" between Thanksgiving and the new year. He told her that an adoptive home study might give him a nice break from his normal routine and because he had the time, he agreed to do it relatively quickly. He scheduled the half a dozen different appointments we needed within a few weeks in Dec and the final appt in early January. When Teri checked with the people in Austin who handled Texas compliance with the Interstate Compact, she learned that this counselor/social worker was on the approved list having completed exactly one year of home study experience in 1965 — twenty years earlier.

Shortly after confirming plans for our home study other things began to happen very quickly. Looking back, we now know that God was answering our prayers when we prayed, "Lord, if this child is to be ours, we ask that you open the doors and help us see that this is your will and if it is not, please let us know by closing the doors." In another call with Becky and Larry we learned that Becky had taken the expectant mother to the hospital for a checkup and she and the baby showed themselves to be in good health. After hearing that we began to become cautiously optimistic that things might be going our way. However, likely because we were not trusting God as completely as we should have, we still did not stop worrying or completely commit to saying we'd adopt the baby. We sort of hedged in our first communications to the birth mother and did not commit to saying we were 100% sure we'd adopt the child. So, we continued to ask God for signs to tell us if we were doing the right thing.

We started the first home study interview in early December, and they seemed to being going well. I had talked with the attorney in downtown Dallas, and he seemed like a nice guy. Then he told me about his non-refundable retainer fee that sort of caught me off guard. So, I hesitated to commit at that point. Seems like this hesitation has started becoming a pattern for me. By the time we went through the Christmas holiday Teri had already made several contacts with one of the two primary points of contact in the Interstate Compact Office in Austin. His name was Clarence, and he was very good at answering her questions and giving her very specific lists of things that we needed to be sure to do. Teri called him several times and Clarence was always patient and detailed in answering her questions. So, Teri had copies of various forms and lists of things to do based on those calls. Here again, we believe it was God's plan that we would get all the information up front from a helpful, friendly Clarence. We never spoke to the other person, a woman who was in charge of the clients whose last name began with M-Z (ours is Y), so she handled our case later and in another surprising twist that God would arrange.

Around Christmas time the counselor/social worker with whom we'd already had our initial interviews, called and asked if he could reschedule the final home interviews with our kids for December 31st instead of January 7th. We agreed to the change, not knowing at the time just how important that would be in God's timing.

After learning that the expectant mother's doctor's visits were going well I had even commented to Teri that if her January 3, 1986 doctor's appointment and planned sonogram went well I would go to the lawyer and pay the retainer to get the process started. Then, the unexpected happened. On December 30th, just before midnight Texas time, we received a call from Larry and Becky telling us they were headed out the door to go pick up the birth mother who was already beginning to go into labor. At fifteen minutes after midnight California time, a nine-pound five-ounce, healthy baby girl was born, underscoring in a dramatic way just how mighty and merciful our God is. Completely free of any deformity or detectable defect, the new baby scored high on the Apgar test given to all infants to detect such things. We felt like this detail was God's way of saying, "See, you don't need to wait on a sonogram. You just need to leave it all to me and trust me." When asked what name they should put on the birth certificate we looked at each other and instantly agreed that she would be Sarah Ruth. We assumed that she would have the birth mother's last name until she was adopted. We later learned that they had put our last name on the birth certificate.

On the morning of December 31, 1985, I called the attorney's office in Dallas to let him know what had happened.

He invited me to me come in later that afternoon without an appointment because of the "unexpected turn of events." Another "God thing" factor was that this attorney had just completed a California to Texas adoption, so he was very familiar with that process and requirements! That trip to Dallas began four of the most action-packed days of my life. The home study was being finished to send to Austin, which was one of the requirements needed before a newborn could legally be released to us and transported to Texas from California. The legal documents that had to be signed by the birth mother, hospital officials, social workers, Interstate Compact offices in California and Texas and by us all had to be drafted.

Meanwhile, we also had to arrange for each of our three other kids to get a physical checkup to satisfy another home study requirement. Amazingly God provided again when we were able to get all three kids doctors' appointments on January 2nd. Also, as had already been pre-arranged, the last home study visit was now also set to happen on December 31st. The social worker arrived at our door that morning to hear the exciting news that our baby had been born! He did the final interviews with each of the kids and looked around our home to check all the physical requirements the house needed to complete home study. He told us that he would have the report ready to send to the Interstate Compact office in Austin the next day. He was good at his word.

On the afternoon of December 31st, I drove to the lawyer's office in Dallas. There I signed the contract and paid the retainer fee, learning they had already begun to prepare to generate all the legal documents. First, he prepared the document Teri would need at the San Diego Hospital to have the child released to her, (after the birth mother also had signed the proper consent forms to satisfy the hospital). He faxed those to the San Diego hospital, so they were waiting when Teri arrived there on January

2nd. On January 1, 1986, I drove Teri to the airport to board a plane to Long Beach, CA, since that was the fastest affordable flight we could book to any airport near San Diego on short notice. She was able to stay with Becky and Larry that night and go to the hospital on January 2nd to meet our new baby. Teri describes walking into the hospital newborn area nervously.

"It was a surreal experience, walking in to pick up my newborn baby!!!. I looked at a whiteboard that had the recent births written down, wondering where my baby was, not seeing the birth mother's name. Then I noticed a separate list of babies on a whiteboard under the heading NIK (No Information Known) which had the birthmother's name. Our Sarah Ruth was not the only baby being given up for adoption then. Because our attorney had faxed over the legal paperwork, I was able to go right into the newborn nursery. The nurses there were very kind and helpful. They took me over to a bassinet in which lay a plump little baby with a lot of black hair. They put her in my arms, and I sat in a rocking chair for a while and just held her and cuddled her and looked at her. By the time I left an hour or so later, I had bonded with this precious gift from the LORD. I loved her just the same as when I first got to know my three previous children I had given birth to! I left the hospital with my beautiful baby girl. I put her in the car seat in the back of the rental car and drove to the Whites' home. Just a humorous note— as I was alone and a bit nervous about the "surrealness" of this experience, I had forgotten to secure the new baby seat I had brought on the plane into the car. I securely strapped Sarah into the baby seat, but as I was driving slowly down the sloped drive away from the hospital and reached the intersection at the bottom and stopped, the car seat with Sarah in it plunked forward into the back of the driver's seat! Yikes! Praise GOD, no harm done! Sarah was secure! I pulled over and strapped that car seat tightly onto the car and proceeded safely our destination."

By January 2nd I (Andy) had picked up all the legal documents from the lawyer and had the completed home study report. I also took all the older kids to their doctor's appointments and got copies of the report on their good health. With those in hand I made a trip to Love Field in Dallas to send the home study report to a friend in Austin who also happened to be our former singles minister at the church where Teri and I met and married. Sherry was living in Austin at that point and planned to receive counter-to-counter parcel delivery via Southwest Airlines. Another requirement for an interstate adoption was that the adopting parents had to have been married for a minimum of two years. Teri and I had just passed our 2nd anniversary on November 23, 1985.

At the same time I was running errands and driving to and from airports our lawyer had also been in communication with the Interstate Compact coordinator in Austin (the lady who handled M-Z) Our attorney had made the comment that he found her to be quite a "bureaucrat" and not overly helpful, which was why we believe God arranged for helpful Clarence to pick up the phone and graciously answer all Teri's questions each time she had called that department earlier! Our attorney had sent her the appropriate legal documents for us. He had also prepared documents for the birth mother which I was to deliver to her in person, have her sign them in the presence of a notary, and bring back to Texas to then send on to Austin. After arranging for our kids to stay with friends, I left for DFW airport on the evening of January 2nd. In the late-night hours of January 2nd, I arrived at the airport in San Diego and drove to Becky and Larry's house where Teri and our new baby were waiting. We met the birth mother there for the first time, sitting at their dining room table, while Sarah was asleep in a bedroom. Larry had arranged for a notary he knew who had recently been involved with a relative's private adoption and had agreed to come to the house late that night to notarize the paperwork. Over the weeks of working with the birth mom, Becky had also shared the gospel with her and befriended her. After some tears and I think some assurance that her child would have a good home, she signed the relinquishment papers and gave us a letter to be opened by Sarah on her 16th birthday.

The next morning, January 3rd, I drove back to San Diego airport to board an early flight back to Dallas. After landing at DFW airport in the early afternoon I drove to Love Field again to send the signed legal documents in a package prepared by the attorney to go to the Interstate Compact officials in Austin. By this time Teri had made arrangements to stay with her cousin who lived near Long Beach, CA , where she would wait until she received official approval to take the baby to Texas on a flight home. While Teri was in California with the baby, I was working directly with our lawyer whose office was in communication with Interstate Compact offices both in Austin and in Sacramento. In Austin our friend Sherry drove downtown to the state office building where the Intestate Compact coordinator was. She helped push the woman Interstate Compact worker, who was in a wheelchair, around from office to office to track town some of the signed forms and correspondence that she could not locate. Even as business hour passed closing time Sherry continued to help find those papers.

Late on that Friday afternoon, January 3, 1986, all the papers were found, and the transfer was approved. Our lawyer confirmed that we had approval from both Sacramento and Austin to bring Sarah Ruth Yates home to Texas. I got the phone call from the lawyer and was overwhelmed by joy as I called and told Teri the news. After preparing the older kids and telling them the news I made a rushed trip to Toys R Us store to buy "baby stuff". That was an amusing shopping trip. I bought diapers and wipes and some other stuff, but I really had no clue.

On Saturday, January 4, 1986, I met Teri and Sarah at the airport and drove them home feeling on top of the world. During that drive home I looked back at the course of the last few weeks and was amazed at all that had occurred. Even now, thirty-eight years later, with Sarah grown and married, we are still in awe of a God that loved us so much and that he was willing to show us repeatedly we could trust Him, even when we kept questioning and doubting. We kept asking and he kept answering with a door opening at just the right time. There is no doubt in our minds that what we started with faltering steps of faith could only have happened because of a faithful, compassionate God who heard our prayers and answered.

2020 Hindsight

When you are tempted to believe that "The Devil is in the details," think about the story of the adoption of baby Sarah. Apparently, God is in the details when it comes to adoption. He was certainly in the details of our adoption into his family. "He predestined us for adoption to sonship through Jesus Christ, in accordance with his pleasure and will." Ephesians 1: 5

It All Began When...

Leaving California

Becky and I began to experience a restlessness about our current situation. We were in a church that was wonderful, unlike any church we had ever experienced in our collective past. I was very much enjoying a ministry like I had never known before. We loved the house and California was a very energizing place to live. Our kids were well situated in their schools. But here was our concern. They were both growing up and did not really have any significant relationship with their grandparents. Our folks, like us, were getting older and we saw that the window of opportunity was getting smaller with the time for them to experience their grandchildren. This surfaced a certain negative note over our otherwise enjoyable life. What were we to do?

The year was 1991 when an associate of John Maxwell's, Bill Phillippe, approached me about a situation he was dealing with in upper South Carolina. Bill was shepherding a church plant near Greenville, S.C., which was in trouble. Somehow my restless situation and his troubled situation came up in a conversation. The idea of me moving to within a few miles of my parents and taking over the troubled church-plant came up.

The idea of leaving a very comfortable and positive place like Skyline and Southern California seemed like a mountain I never wanted to cross. But the restlessness continued to grow. We continued to pray and talk about a possible move back to the Southeast.

There is a fundamental component to my make-up: I always want to keep growing. And getting in touch with that personal passion became a source compelling me to open the door to this major transition. I had grown immensely under the leadership of first Chuck Shores and of course, John Maxwell. Of course, I must include the completion of the master's in divinity at Bethel-west as a strong contribution to my growth. But now I felt that I needed a new challenge. The prospect of taking on a church plant was becoming singularly appealing.

So, in February 1992, driving a loaded 24-foot U-Haul followed by Becky, the kids, Noni, (you may recall her from chapter 21) and our family cat, Chrissy, in the Dodge Caravan we headed East. Somewhere in the desert of Arizona with the windows down, Chrissy decided she had had enough of the trip and took a mighty leap to exit through the window. Noni was quick. She grabbed the cat's tail and brought her safely back inside. I doubt Chrissy appreciated the rescue but had that not happened she would have cashed in on what remained of her 9 lives. She would have long been lost among the Joshua trees and cacti, then be eventually devoured by a coyote. And we would have been plagued with a terribly remorseful Elizabeth. She would even weep profusely at the death of a goldfish.

When we finally arrived safely in South Carolina, our first order of business was to find housing. It didn't happen quickly so in the meantime we camped out with my parents who lived about thirty miles from Powdersville in Clemson. Our search for housing was naturally nearer the church. What resulted immediately got our kids closer to my parents and that lasted 3 months. For those 3 months Chrissy hid out in my parents' basement traumatized by her transition from California.

My parents put up with it a lot. It was not a totally pleasant situation and certainly stretched all six of us as we learned to live together. But eventually, we were able to purchase our new home in Moonville, about 10 miles from Friendship Wesleyan.

To say Friendship was a drastic contrast to Skyline Wesleyan is an understatement. The church was on the very northern edge of Anderson County backing up to Greenville County. It seemed there were churches on every corner, mostly Baptist. In fact, there was a Baptist church that rented space from the backside of Friendship's property. I once said to Pastor Jim Tippens, the Baptist pastor, "If I were going to plant a Baptist church in this community, I know what I would name it."

When Jim asked me my name choice, I said, "Yet Another Baptist Church."

One of the changes in my ministry at Friendship was preaching. I had preached to the singles at Skyline, but my teaching had been overshadowed by the able communication skills of John Maxwell. That served to sharpen me. When I was preparing to leave, John had encouraged me to take tapes of as many of his sermons as possible, which I did. He told me to use any of his messages and he would not even expect credit.

I tried that for a short while but found that my own "preaching muscles" were growing weak. I went back to preparing my own sermons and I found my style to be relying on highly illustrative lessons.

One such sermon was based on Paul's writing in Philippians 3 where he contrasted his new life in Christ with his old life in Judaism. He considered his prior accomplishments as "rubbish." To bring this point home, I placed a large trash can on the stage and threw into it trophies, awards, diplomas, money and other items that we believe give us significance. But of course, for the believer these things are garbage in contrast to knowing Jesus.

As the congregation left the service, a young special needs man pulled me aside and whispered in my ear, "Pastor Larry, if Paul doesn't want those things, do you think I could have them?"

It certainly proved he was listening, but I was quite stumped as to how to answer his request.

I had only been at Friendship Wesleyan a short time when a lady named Emily contacted me to reach out to her friend Preston. She had been praying for him for years and he had a store within a very easy walk of Friendship. I promised I would but inwardly I chaffed at the prospect. That kind of targeted evangelism was always awkward at best and usually a dead end. But I knew that to create a new congregation would mean I needed to make as many contacts as possible in the community.

I learned from Emily that Preston was a man who had run pornographic video stores in the area. He had publicly appeared in the news defending his right to market his videos. But he eventually was shut down and now owned this little establishment behind our church that rented legitimate movies along with a limited amount of electronic equipment including televisions.

We needed a new T.V. in our home so I went into the store to check its deals. In that context, I got to know Preston. I was relieved over the few times I went into his store that the subject of who I was and what I did never came up.

Over time I learned more and more about him. He was currently single but was managing 4 kids that lived with him. I also learned that in addition to his current merchandise he rented equipment for parties, including a dunking booth. He was quite a wheeler-dealer. So much so that I bought a new television from him.

Eventually, he asked me more about myself. He learned that I was the pastor of the church within view of his establishment, that I was new in the area and had moved there from Southern California. He said, "I'll need to come and visit your church sometime." I think it was a matter of reciprocity.

Shortly after that comment, he did come and visit and shortly after that visit I was able to share the gospel with him. He trusted Christ. Shortly after that the subject of baptism was broached and he was ready. He only had one request, could he be baptized in his dunking booth?

That designated Sunday came. The booth was set up on the lawn between the church and the strip mall that contained his store. We set up chairs and we worshipped outdoors. The weather was perfect. His children attended and Preston's baptism was covered in the local weekly paper. The publicity certainly helped to put Friendship Wesleyan in the minds of some in the community.

The unique baptism led to another request from Preston. He was very repentant from the very public stance he had taken when he ran his pornographic video stores. He wanted somehow to communicate his changed life to the community he offended. I learned that he still had in his possession the X-rated videos. I told him about the burning of the New Age material that Noni had brought to my office years ago at Skyline.

He came back later and suggested we do the same thing in a very public way with his scandalous movies. I was reluctant. How could we engage the community in such an event? We were a small church with at best 60 in attendance. We had little influence. Preston came back with a plan for publicity. We would set a date and with a list of media outlets, he said he would do the work of communicating about the evening set in early November. With that promise we proceeded.

When the evening came, it was cold and windy, but no precipitation. Every media outlet had been alerted. We also had to curtail the plan to burn the videos. The plastic in their casing had made them toxic and to burn them would be a violation of EPA rules. In addition to the videos Preston had pornographic magazines so that constituted the fire. To abolish the movies, we equipped the small group of church folks with hammers, and they proceeded to burst apart the films. (The kids loved the destructive task).

And the major local media outlets showed up. Our "burn" was featured on the 11 o'clock news on every tv outlet. The Greenville News, the primary newspaper in the area, made it a front-page story with a full color picture. And every radio station that had a local news broadcast covered the story. It was amazing! At nearby Clemson University, a student generated "rag," took a very dim view of the event comparing it to book burning of books in Nazi Germany. They had a picture of me and a quote that cast me as much as they could to Hitler. Instead of infuriating me, I was amused. I felt the smile of God's approval.

20/20 Hindsight

Even though I obeyed God's call and left California, the same God was in South Carolina. Following Him and following his will means living in His joy and approval. But it is not always easy.

It All Began When...

Bradley

Bradley, our son, was set to go into his senior year. In many ways he was coasting along, and for the most part that pleased us. He enjoyed engaging with his peers including the ones from Friendship and the Greenville First Wesleyan, close by. He did give us trouble at home, but that was not anything new. On the other hand, we received only a few complaints from his high school. His grades were not great, yet his attitude and behavior toward us, particularly toward his mom was getting more and more difficult. He often stole money out of her purse. That had gone on for a long time and we brought corrections again and again.

I have clued you in to the fact that Bradley is a twin. His twin brother, (not identical) had been adopted by a wonderful Christian couple in California but they had moved to Arizona. We kept in touch with them and on rare occasions in the early years we had gotten the boys together. Neither particularly asked for those reunions. Their last time to see each other was on our journey east from California. We stopped in for a visit.

His twin brother had become more and more out of control. His parents had come to point of having to place him in a small rural Christian school in Louisiana. In the back of our mind that option seemed like an undesirable but necessary possibility if Bradley's behavior grew more out of control.

Naturally, he wanted to get his driver's license. Having him drive was appealing to us but also posed some frightening prospects. We agreed to sign off him taking the driver's test provided he was able to pass the drug test. We couldn't help but wonder if he was a user. I told him that both the drug test and the driver's test would come together, and he needed to prepare for such an occasion that would come unannounced.

In the meantime, Becky and I explored the school where his brother was placed, should he fail the drug test. He was marginally aware of our planning. He had grown so preoccupied with a group of teenagers that were able to pick him up and take him on weekend excursions. Of course, he was under a curfew that he resisted but managed to keep.

The school said "yes" to accepting Bradley should the need arise, and we admitted him with a clear understanding of the parameters they set. We understood that once he was admitted it would be a yearlong stay. We would only be able to communicate with him by mail, interspersed with a phone call we would initiate once a month. In addition to the schooling, he would be living and working on the school's farm.

He did fail the drug test and we put our plan into action. Details are not to be included except to say, we were on our way to Louisiana in the Dodge Caravan with him, along with his clothes and some personal items. He slept in the back seat only waking up in Atlanta, where he began to question where we were going. We broke it to him, and he reacted by begging and pleading to go back home. The fact that he would be in school with his brother meant little to him.

That was hard. Becky and I had reasoned between ourselves; to take this tough stand was a clear attempt to turn him around from the direction he was headed. We felt strongly. "This is an option that has presented itself. In a year, we don't want to look back and deeply wish we had made this choice."

We drove away from his new school with heavy hearts but confident we had made the right decision. It wasn't long before we realized the benefit of our hard choice. Twice during that year, we had to tell Bradley how two of his friends that he hung out with had been killed in two separate auto accidents. Each time he would say, "If I had been there, it is likely I would have been in the car with them."

Additionally, he quickly came to appreciate the school including the discipline he was undergoing. He said little about his brother and it was a few months into his time that his brother chose to leave but Bradley endured the year and received his high school diploma. We drove down to Louisiana to bring him back home.

His return brought us a son who was very respectful and compliant. It was wonderful. His next plan was to enroll at nearby Southern Wesleyan University (formerly Central Wesleyan). We scrapped money together to get him into his first semester there, living in the men's dorm. He went with the understanding that to continue that education he would need to work and help pay his way.

To facilitate that, Preston, my wheeler dealer friend, helped me to purchase a small clunker of car so that he could drive to a job. He secured a part-time job at a nearby grocery store. Things were set and we were so happy for these developments.

School started in late August, but by early October everything had unraveled. We learned that he had taken the car we provided and had disappeared. The grocer had heard nothing from him, and the school said they had not seen him in three weeks. We had no choice but to wait until he resurfaced.

And he resurfaced in the Pickens's County Jail. He had taken the car we provided, reconnected with an old friend and together they went on a stealing spree, breaking and entering businesses. They were finally apprehended when they broke into a music store in Easley right across from the donut shop while cops watched. It probably was the easiest arrest they had ever made. And certainly, if they attempted a get-away in the little car they were driving, it would have been like chasing Fred Flintstone and Barney Rubble.

I made my way to the Sheriff's office with additional evidence I had to turn into him implicating my son. I certainly was not there to plead for him and post bail. I had told Bradley all his years in school that if he was guilty and in trouble at school, he was also in trouble with me and his mom. Bailing him out was no option.

The Sheriff undoubtedly didn't expect what I did. He said, "I wish there were more parents like you."

Bradley was sentenced to incarceration for a year in the South Carolina Youth division. Becky says reflectively that whole episode was one of the most difficult times in her life. We went, but she hated visiting Bradley in prison.

Amazingly, the leadership of Friendship Wesleyan stood with us. They were great when they could have taken a very different tact.

20/20 Hindsight

Paul wrote to Timothy regarding the selection of church overseers "He must manage his family well." (I Timothy 3:4) Managing a family well is not perfection but choosing to respond in a loving strong way to when infractions arise. Apparently, the congregation at Friendship Wesleyan saw it that way.

It All Began When...

Willow Creek

I received a voice mail from Sheryl Fleisher asking me to call her back. I served on staff at Skyline with Sheryl and we had lost contact over the past five years. We worked hard at Skyline. The demand on our time coupled with our personal intensity to ministry had meant that we had not much more contact outside of our perspective focuses. I deeply respected her great leadership. Naturally I wondered, "Why would she be calling me?"

When I returned her call, I learned that she was no longer at Skyline but had taken a position as an Area Director at Willow Creek Community Church outside of Chicago. I was marginally familiar with Willow Creek. I knew it was considered one of the premier churches in the country with a massive attendance (17,000 every weekend). I had heard its founding pastor, Bill Hybels, when he came as a guest speaker at a leadership conference at Skyline. I knew it's amazing inception and incredible rapid growth.

Sheryl was new there on staff and her oversight was to Single Adults. Sheryl was recruiting leadership to come and join her there and she thought of me. I was honored to say the least. And I was overwhelmed with the prospect of serving on such a huge staff but even more overwhelmed at the prospect of leaving Friendship. After five years we were around 100 in attendance. That represented much diligent work, and I was deeply invested in this little flock and the community they came from. How could I possibly leave them?

Detailing the process of the decision would prove to be tedious. It was also immensely painful. The worst pain was the prospect of leaving the flock at Friendship. But then the process was fraught with challenges. Not only Willow checking me out, but I was checking out Willow Creek. I was awed by what I saw and learned.

While we were there, John Maxwell was the guest speaker at the midweek service. I remember him issuing a strong challenge to take big risk for the sake of the gospel and the Kingdom of God. I felt he was speaking to me, but he didn't know Becky and I were there until after the service. I told him his message was directed at me and it had helped me turn the corner on saying yes to this new challenge before me.

My last interview at Willow Creek was with an Elder. She had asked me about my conversion story, and I shared with her about my coming to Christ as a sophomore in college.

Then she asked about my baptism. I was baptized at age 13 with the rest of the boys in my junior high Sunday school class. Sadly, there were no real teaching offered to us boys about the significance of baptism that I can recall. It was just the next thing the church expected of us, and we all took the step.

After hearing my disjointed journey, the Elder responded, "You have not experienced believers' baptism."

I agreed. She only told me what I had known for some time but I had lacked the will or opportunity to rectify my situation. It had been my fantasy that my believer's baptism would take place in the Jordan River where Jesus was baptized. But as of this writing, such a trip had never happened.

Then she said, "When we have our next baptism service in June, would you be willing to be baptized?"

Without hesitation, I said, "Yes."

That promise was kept and when the day came, without even knowing this was going to take place, my parents drove up from South Carolina to Illinois and witnessed my baptism. Yet, it was awkward when individuals who knew I was on staff asked why I was baptized, and I had to tell them the truth about my history. But telling my baptism story has helped several times for others to catch the significance of believer's baptism.

To rush this up, we left to return to South Carolina excited about the prospect of moving to Chicago. It was exciting, scary, and sad. The process of transition came to us as another mountain to move, and it was. It was October, and our move was to happen at the turn of the year 1998.

The to do list was daunting:

1. Putting the house on the market
2. Telling our parents
3. Telling our friends
4. Telling our Friendship family
5. Packing
6. Moving
7. Finding new housing in Schaumburg/Barrington

Each hurdle brought new waves of grief. I was still grieving when we arrived in snowy Illinois in late January 1998. This chapter could go on for a long time but from the list I want to share about the sale of our house. We decided to market it ourselves. The market was not good, especially in the late fall and winter.

After putting the "For Sale by Owner" sign in front of our house by the end of October almost immediately a couple wanted to see our house. The state of South Carolina had notified them that their house was in the path of a new highway coming through, so they knew they had to move. They didn't know when. They loved our place, but they were not ready to buy. After that initial burst of interest, nothing more happened. NOTHING! We busied ourselves with the other items on the list.

The New Year came and nothing new developed. I called the original couple who were interested and nothing new had changed with them but their interest in our house had increased, so much so they hinted that they might apply for a loan if the mortgage company would take into consideration the state's intention of taking their house. They promised to explore that possibility.

We continued to pack and prepare to move. Oh yes, and we prayed and prayed.

One very good development came during our preparation to move. Bradley was released from prison. We invited him to move with us, but he was fortunate enough to have a job that paid well enough for him to rent his own apartment. We helped him furnish it with items from our house. He seemed very set to take on life without us close by.

When mid-January came, the perspective buyers were ready to make an offer. Which we readily accepted. Papers were signed, the moving van was packed, and we made our way to Chicago-HOUSE SOLD!

20/20 Hindsight

Waiting patiently on God is not a passive proposition. Waiting involves doing what is necessary as you anticipate the answer coming through.

It All Began When..

A Day Alone with God

Sheryl Fleisher, my Divisional Leader, introduced our team of Single Adult leaders to Ruth Barton. Ruth was the head of her own ministry named Transformation Center. The focus was equipping church leadership through spiritual disciplines that would bring about a deep heart connection with God. In retrospect, I had a very limited exposure to spiritual disciplines. Since first coming to Christ, I had struggled to practice daily devotions, personal Bible study and prayer. What I had put into practice for years was faithful church attendance and fellowship.

Early on in my walk with God I had learned about experiencing a day Alone with God through a little booklet published by the Navigators, "How to Spend a Day Alone with God." Over the years I had sought monthly to put that into practice. Ruth had learned through a year of training with spiritual guides to bring such a practice into focus. She taught us about the practice of Solitude and Silence. It took what I had already experienced and took me deeper.

In Warrenville, about an hour from Willow Creek, I discovered a wonderful retreat named Cynical. I continued my monthly days alone with the Lord. There was never a better place to get alone and seek God. (Frankly, I have not found a place that has even come close to that location.)

Ruth's influence had encouraged me to believe that experiencing a dynamically alive presence with God is not only possible, but it is to be the focus of our very lives. He loves us and he wants to show up in our experience in vibrant ways. Yes, I had had such experiences in the past, but they were largely in the context of ministry. The thrill of my life was, and still is, to see God use me. But just to know Him through a personal spiritual discipline did not happen as readily.

Through Ruth's influence my expectations began to change. I can never forget a visit to Cynical where Jesus came to the room where I was silently waiting. (I share this story with some of the same constraint similar to how Paul shared his visit into the third heaven experience in II Corinthians 12). I am not interested in putting myself in the light of someone unique and special. I believe Jesus wants to be real with anyone who is willing to seek him. This is not a cause for bragging.

I had settled into the quiet little room that was provided by Cynical. I was not at all physically tired or sleepy. When the afternoon came on a day of solitude and silence, I would usually battle that. However, I was quite alert when I stretched out across the bed to be open to God. I had laid there for about 10 minutes when suddenly, I became very aware that I was no longer alone in the room. Jesus had joined me.

Did I see Him with my physical eyes? No. But I did sense Him in a more overt way than I had ever sensed Him before. When I was new in my faith I used to go on walks at night in quiet, unpopulated portions of my neighborhood. I loved to talk to Him out loud, inviting Him to walk beside me. I often thought of Him as a bigger and older brother that I had often longed to have. Those walks and conversations were enjoyable. And during my time alone with Him that morning, the same rich awareness that I had experienced years ago came back, only stronger. He sat down on the side of the bed where I lay and invited me to place my head on his lap. He gently stroked my head and told me how precious I was to Him. I felt completely loved. He talked to me about the wonderful way He planned to use me in the future. Details of the latter part of this experience are strong in my memory but what I understood Him to be saying is still more like to me a dream than a reality. I prefer not to go into them now.

I was weeping tears of joy as I became totally relaxed in His presence. The whole experience sadly faded after about an hour. I continued to remain still and quiet in the room reflecting on what had happened there. I believed that it was simply a gift of God to me that has become such a deep reference point for the things that would happen to me not long into the future.

I have not had such an identical experience again, nor do I seek it. I would certainly welcome it. This experience brought balance to my faith, and it has caused me to value the Word of God in my heart. The promises of God in scripture have become more valuable to me than the amazing time I had in that room in Warrenville, Illinois. Yet I am grateful for both.

20/20 Hindsight

Jesus said to the Pharisees, "You study the Scriptures diligently because you think that in them you have eternal life. These are the very scriptures that testify of me." (John 5: 39). The knowledge of God's Word may keep us from experiencing the living reality of Jesus.

It All Began When....

September 11

I was in the kitchen preparing breakfast when Becky called from the bedroom, "Turn on the Today Show." With the urgency in her voice, I rushed to the tv in the living room and quickly found the NBC affiliate in Chicago. On the screen I saw, as Becky joined me, the burning of the World Trade Center and shortly later the second tower being clobbered by another jet. She had heard in the bedroom a radio report of the news which alerted her to get me to the television.

We watched as others did that morning of September 11, 2001; the tragic events unfolded before us. Most of our plans for that day and for several days to follow became frozen in time. Even later that morning when I went to my chiropractic appointment, the doctor and I sat and watched what was happening on the news. Everything became distant and surreal.

How little did I know that my own plans would be so radically altered because of this day a year later. Willow Creek Community Church was not hit by the jets that devastated the World Trade Towers or the Pentagon, but the finances of this hugely successful church were devastated by an economy crippled by those events.

Surrounding this world class church were major cooperations who were now suffering greatly from the effects of September 11. United Airlines, Motorola, Sears, and others that were headquartered within a few miles of the church were forced to lay off high level employees, many of which attended and gave to Willow. By the end of the year Willow was also faced with the troubling task of downsizing.

For weeks the staff, numbering 400, had gathered in the chapel to be updated about the pending situation. It was always couched in terms of "We hope it does not come to this." Each meeting was sobering, and I personally wavered between dread and denial. Could I possibly be one of the ones who would be let go? I pushed it aside by rationalizing. Because Elizabeth was a senior in high school, how could I be severed from a job I had had for four years?

I am going to depart from this tale to talk about Elizabeth. It had been very hard on her to move to Chicago. A few months into our new location she enrolled at Schaumburg High School. Prior to this she had attended near our church in Powdersville, a small school where Becky taught 4th grade. Now she has been thrust into a huge school of over 2000 youth from very diverse backgrounds. It was hard on her.

She had loved Willow Creek and had been very active in its gigantic and exciting youth program. We felt that one of the great benefits of coming to Willow had been her being able to gain such a wonderful exposure to the Lord though this ministry.

With great sadness and alarm, we discovered that Elizabeth was getting swallowed up by her peer world rather than the kids whom she had met in church. I had just assumed that having such a rich spiritual advantage was taking care of her spiritual life and I had grown lax, to say it bluntly, about attending to her growth in the Lord.

What happened in our home was more alarming than the attack of September 11. Elizabeth announced to her mom and I that she no longer believed what we believed, and she would not be attending church anymore. My immediate reaction was a calm, "You don't have to believe what we believe but you do have to attend church." I clarified. There were three opportunities each week for attendance. The youth program, weekend church and Wednesday or Thursday night New Community. The New Community service was an exuberant time of worship followed by deep Bible teaching. She would have to attend two of the three.

I felt sure she would pick the youth meeting for one of the three. Instead, she picked both meetings where Becky and I were in attendance. She would go with us. I watched her week after week sit through those meetings uninvolved. Her body language was a loud, "I'm not here." It broke our hearts, but we only hoped something of God was getting through.

Her behavior at home was also difficult and her preoccupation with her secular friends became even more involved. The worst was that she developed a relationship with a young man out of high school. Controlling that relationship was very difficult. Like her brother, we exercised a curfew, which she kept. It seemed like the only thing that we had to reel her in. It was hard.

When January 2002 came, the management of Willow Creek told the staff they would be calling individually about 33 staff into a personal meeting to communicate their decision as to whether they would be laid off. We were to be in our office available should we be one of the ones called. What a nerve-racking day.

I got two calls that day. One was from South Carolina telling me that Bradley and his wife Tristan had given birth to a little girl they named Izabella. The second call came for me to come to a location to talk with one of Willow's administrators. He informed me of the decision concerning my future with the church. He informed me of my downsizing. I don't know if he himself knew at that time but soon, Willow would be downsizing the Single's Ministry. My time at Willow would end February 15. I would be given a severance package that would be good until May. My health insurance would continue until June. I was encouraged that if I had anything to communicate with Bill Hybels, the senior and founding pastor, his office was open to me anytime that day if I wished to talk with him.

I didn't cry until I was met by a fellow staffer, Marie Shepherd. She stood waiting outside the little office where I was informed of the severance. She opened her arms for me to weep. Rejection hurts. I was so grateful for the rich comfort and prayer she provided me.

Then I went up to Bill Hybels's office. As sad as I felt, I also felt a huge burst of gratitude. I told him I was so grateful for the 4 years that I had gotten to be a part of the whole experience of being in this church. He also prayed for me and promised to write a letter of reference for me to enable me to get into my next position.

As I shared my hurt and disappointment, I was also able to share how God had blessed us with a new, first time ever grandchild. Her name is Izabella.

20/20 Hindsight

God's timing is always right. With great pain he also brings great consolation.

It All Began When…

Wheaton, Maryland

I was rushing out of the house to go to take a test to be a school bus driver and the phone rang. Being unemployed was a new experience. I had jobs since I was 14 when I worked at Mack's Variety and Fashion as a stockboy. Now here I am 54 years old without work. After my father retired, he drove a school bus and loved it. I could do that too and it would give me time to pursue new work. But first I had to pass the test to be a driver.

On the phone was my friend Steve Wright. He pastored Oaklawn Wesleyan Church over an hour away. I had called sometime earlier and left a brief message telling him to pray for my status.

He called back getting right to the matter at hand, "What is going on?"

As I gave him the thumbnail news of my situation, I had begun by telling him I would like to give him an explanation face to face soon since I was on my way out for the bus driving exam. Then I told him the story of being rifted from Willow. He listened with empathy.

Then he said, "You are not going to be a school bus driver. I want to meet you and discuss hiring you part-time to assist me here at Oaklawn. Let's set up a time to discuss that."

When we met a few days later I found myself back at work twice a week for Steve with responsibilities that included joining a work team traveling to Georgia to do sheet rocking at an orphanage, do visitation to shut-ins from the church, and even some preaching a few times. We switched our Sunday attendance from Willow to Oaklawn.

In addition, I was for the first time in my life seriously constructing a resume and learning to pursue jobs over the internet and the phone. Because of my ministry history, I had almost two phone interviews a week and one in person interview in Georgia while I was on the work detail with the men from Oaklawn.

It was at a Willow Creek associated church that was growing rapidly. An interesting thing happened while the pastor left me alone briefly. His associate with tears in her eyes told me, "You don't want to work here. I can't last here much longer because the workload is so difficult. I have been robbed of my personal life trying to meet the demands." She indicated that the problem was the expectations of the pastor. I completed the interview graciously, but knowing we would not be moving to Georgia.

The prospect of moving back to the Southeast was certainly appealing. A church staff position had been passed on to me in Greenville. Excitedly, I had told my dad to pray for the phone interview that was coming up. That interview, although very pleasant had turned out to be a dead end when the subject of women in ministry had come up. I had no qualms about women in ministry, and they certainly did. But it also was a double dead end. After my phone call with my father, he called back to discourage me from returning to Greenville because of Bradley.

Bradley, although married and a father, had become more and more out of control with his drug abuse. He had spent more time incarcerated and certainly that had greatly impacted on his own family. As far as I know that problem had not directly impacted Mom and Dad. They lived some 50 miles away. But Dad understood from living life that addiction had a way of creating dependencies that could well impact my family. I was so grateful for his wisdom.

A Baptist church on the Maryland side of Washington D.C. had picked up my resume online and I was first aware of their interest when I received an internet inquiry from a Dr. Ed Williams. He and his wife were coming to a conference at Willow Creek. They requested to meet me.

I could sometimes tell something is God's will when I find myself kicking and screaming. That was certainly my experience with every other major move in my life. I responded to the inquiry by saying I would be willing to meet but I wanted to say up front that I didn't want to be in the D.C. area, nor did I want to be a Baptist and I really didn't want to be in a church where the minister was called doctor. (I didn't immediately realize I was already kicking and screaming.)

The pastor promptly responded. "They don't call me Dr. Williams; they call me Eddie. And there are plans to change the name of our church soon and we will be dropping Baptist from our name."

A word about my resistance to being a Baptist. I initially got that from my dad who was raised Baptist but had chosen to become affiliated with the Wesleyan Church. The perception was passed on to me that Baptist were lacking in an emphasis of living a holy life. I've already written about the legalism I experienced growing up that I had rejected. Except for the somewhat irrational reaction to identifying as a Baptist, the issue of the differences between the two-church grouping faded for the most part. I was soon to learn that there were some positives about the Baptists.

Eddie and I met, and we talked for several hours. He filled me in on the congregation, the vision for the future, the culture of the church and surrounding community. We compared our personal journeys, and I was able to share with him the experiences with both of our children. (He was supportive). There was hardly any subject we didn't cover that three hours would allow. We both enjoyed the conversation. It ended with him inviting Becky and me to come to First Baptist Church of Wheaton, Maryland for a June visit. We accepted.

Mary Beth Williams picked us up at Reagan National Airport. Becky and I had visited Washington D.C. separately years before. In college I had been very active in the College Republicans and twice traveled to the Capital including riding on the South Carolina Float as a Colonial soldier in Nixon's Inaugural parade. At that time, I had aspired to go into politics and maybe one day live there. But my coming to follow Jesus had long ago taken away that desire.

First Baptist Church of Wheaton was set in an urban area with around 250 in attendance. The primary uniqueness was its diversity, like the community where it was situated. Diversity was a growing value for me. The primary appeal for the church position I had interviewed for in Georgia had been its diversity. And in retrospect, I had not unpacked when I told the story in chapter 22 about my encounter with Jesus, but he had given me an inkling of a vision that involved diversity.

The job that I was being asked to serve was simply an associate staff filling in a slot that had been held by a husband and wife who were responding to a call to move back to their home area of Texas. It would be taking the roles of community care and discipleship. I could pick the title I would like. I liked the title "Pastor of Spiritual Formation." I accepted the position, and they accepted me. The official start date would be September 1, giving us the summer to sell our Illinois house and find a home in Maryland.

Amazingly during that summer Becky and I celebrated our 25ᵗʰ anniversary. We were able to go back to San Diego and have a reunion with the Skyline Singles down on the Bay. We felt so loved and appreciated. It was immensely healing following the painful separation from Willow Creek

20/20 Hindsight

Why is kicking and screaming so much a part of a call from God? Does it have to be? It comes from my tendency to cling on to the past and to love so deeply those God has brought in our lives. The antidote is to anticipate Heaven, the greatest reunion of all.

It All Began When…

Leaving Chicago Behind

Pastor Steve took it on himself to help Elizabeth into Anderson College in Indiana. He had connections and felt strongly that the best place for her to be in a Christian College, rather than being left behind in Chicago. I couldn't agree more. She couldn't agree less. She was graduating from high school, had a job and a boyfriend and at 18 was ready to set out on her own. She was even getting some credit at the local community college.

Steve, using his connections, was able to get her admitted, despite her poor performance in high school. With her in tow, we visited Anderson, but she was underwhelmed to say the least. She reluctantly went along with plans to sign up for a dorm room and I was able to secure a student loan.

Everything was in place for us to drive her to her new venture and in the morning, we were to leave. She had spent the night with a girlfriend, promising to show up in time for the trip, but instead I got an adamant email saying she would not be going. Her plan was to stay behind when we moved and continue in the direction she wanted for her life. Her plan won out, much to our huge disappointment.

She had joined us in July when we went to Maryland to look for housing. In the heat we spent two weeks looking at

house after house we could afford. None were suitable. The
market was fast paced, and the options were few. We returned
to Illinois very discouraged.

We were officially to be back to Silver Spring Labor Day
weekend. Our house had sold, furnishings were in storage. We
drove to Maryland leaving Elizabeth behind and reservations
to stay in a Residence Inn for a month.

After the service at First Baptist of Wheaton that first
Sunday our realtor called very excited about an open house,
she felt was perfect for us and in our price range. We had to
move quickly. After our visit to the location, we agreed with
her assessment, and we made an offer. Based on the volume
of others viewing the location, we knew that ours would not
be the only offer and they would be quite competitive, so I
suggested that we offer $10,000 over the asking price. Then I
felt rather impulsively that we needed to up that offer by $100.

Later that evening our realtor called to tell us that our
offer had been accepted and it was the $100 that made the
difference. As we signed the papers closing the deal, the seller's
realtor said she had never seen a sale take place where the margin
of the deal was so small. I felt confident it had been a stroke
of wisdom from the Holy Spirit, not my genius that came up
with the plus $100 offer.

We lived in that home in Silver Spring for 19 years. It was
the longest we had ever lived in one house in our married life.

We moved in the Silver Spring house in October and 3 days
later the area we had moved to was besieged by what became
known as the D.C. sniper. We learned later that one of our
neighbor's brothers had been one of the first killed.

We also learned that our neighborhood was very diverse.
Next door there was a Hispanic family. Across the street was
a Jewish couple. A Vietnamese family lived around the corner

and down the street lived an Indian couple. A family from Bangladesh had moved in not long after we did within eyesight of our front door. We loved the variety.

Our church was not quite as diverse but more so than any church we had ever attended. It was clearly in transition as many of the old attendees had left due to the departure from hymns and organ music to guitars, drums, and praise music. The congregation, though still a blending of ages, was becoming younger.

And the move to change its name was underway. The Sunday morning when the vote was to be taken, I had invited a young Nigerian man to the service. He came in his native garb.

The sanctuary was unusually full, and the energy was higher than normal. Those who were members were asked to remain after the service. I said goodbye to my guest explaining what was going to happen next. I never saw him again.

After some passionate debate where one older man stood and announced, "I'm proud to be a Baptist." The vote proceeded. The decision to change the name was soundly defeated. I learned later that the "proud Baptist" had rallied disenfranchised members who had not attended the church, in some cases years, to come and vote. They did vote, and after voting, they never returned.

I was disappointed, but Eddie framed it as my first test of my calling to Wheaton. I certainly was far too in to back out.

20/20 Hindsight

John Maxwell used to say, "How do you know a person is called? They don't quit."

It All Began When...

The Fellowship of the Called

Paula Moutsos, a young black woman who I had gotten to know at First Baptist, spoke to me in the Welcome Time of a church service. (Welcome Time was a regular feature of our congregation when we took time in the middle of a Sunday morning to greet others in attendance). I knew that Paula and her husband had come to Christ at FBCW before we arrived, and she was one of several chefs who attended our church. She worked in the kitchen at the White House.

For reasons I don't need to go into now, I found myself abruptly saying to her, "Paula, why are you using your hands to make a living when you are so gifted using your voice." Paula possessed such a winning way of wording ideas. I had witnessed her speak with such clarity and insight.

That question resulted in her eventually leaving her job as a chef and enrolling at Bethel Seminary east. She was responding to a possible call from God to go into full time Christian Ministry.

It became my purpose early in my time at Wheaton to discover individuals who were sensing such a call, form them into a small group and help them discover indeed what God was asking of them. Paula was the first to join this group.

I regularly prayed with Carol. I did that for several reasons. Our prayer time was early Sunday morning along with a few others. Carol Campbell originally from Jamaica, was a powerful prayer warrior and I clearly learned more from her, more than she did from me. But she had expressed that she wondered if God was calling her into full time ministry. I Invited her to join F.O.T.C. (Fellowship of the Called)

The third member was Josh Bailey. Josh, a twenty something military man had come to live with us, renting out our basement. Initially Josh was only going to be with us for a few months until he married a young woman in Tennessee. We were able to provide him with housing until the wedding so that he wouldn't have to renew the lease on his apartment.

During those few months Josh and I had many deep conversations about marriage that came out of the years of pre-marital counseling I did in California. We also talked about ministry, and he sensed maybe that was a call on his life. Certainly, with the fluctuation regarding his future, he felt it best to call off his engagement.

Not only did he join the F.O.T.C. group, but he ended up living with us in our home for the next 5 years. He became like a son to us. The local newspaper called my office prior to Father's Day one year and asked if I knew of a father/son relationship in which the relationship was not biological but social. I suggested the relationship between Josh and myself. This resulted in the paper doing a story on us including a picture they took at our house.

There were several others who initially started the group, like Mike Thompson. Mike and his wife Debbie lived up the street from us, and not long after we moved in had given his life to Christ, got baptized and joined the church. He was a nurse. Even though he had not expressed a possible call to Christian ministry but because of his spiritual hunger to grow and his living so close by, I invited him into the group.

There were other criteria that I exercised in committing my time to a person but there is no higher quality I look for than teachability-a hunger to learn and grow and that hunger is matched with a desire to be used by God. Each of the F.O.T.C. participants exhibited such hunger.

Of those who participated, as of this writing, only Paula went on to become a paid minister. She took my place on staff in 2012 when I retired from the church.

Josh later married a young woman from our church, and he did go to Bethel Seminary in St. Paul but is serving the Lord with Ruthie and their little daughter in the Minneapolis area as a lay person. He is very gifted in IT and has benefited me in the work I was called to after retirement.

Carol was called some years later after F.O.T.C. to the highest of calling. She succumbed to cancer and now is serving Jesus on location in Heaven.

Mike and Debbie moved out of state, and until his recent passing we remained connected by the internet.

2020 Hindsight

From way back in Crusade days, the purpose of my life is multiplication. Paula is a prime example of how that took place. Thankfully she is not the only one.

It All Began When...

M.U.M

I pulled Eddie aside and said, "I want to run something by you that is on my heart." Characteristically, he listened intently. I had been feeling a new restlessness. And if I were to trust that restlessness it would result in taking me off the staff of what was now called, "Streams of Hope." (First Baptist Church of Wheaton had to change its name. The building had sold, and we had migrated north of Wheaton to a location nearby Olney, Maryland. Our old name was inaccurate.) The property was bought for the old location, and we were temporarily sharing a beautiful structure serving a Christian school. The church was renamed, and plans were underway to take up permanent residence in Olney.

I was a few months from retirement and with all the transitions, my role felt less and less beneficial to the congregation. When I thought about retiring, I had no plans or desire to play golf and fish and I felt that I was energetic and healthy enough not to hang up work.

I will digress to say a year after moving to Maryland I did undergo double bypass surgery, but my annual heart test showed I was even doing well enough to continue playing my favorite sport of racquetball. I wanted to continue to be productive.

Afterall Becky was still working. I wanted to work too, but no longer at the church.

I had become aware of a part-time job opening in Wheaton. The Director of Mid-county United Ministries was retiring. Very early in my time in Wheaton, I met Diane Schroeder and M.U.M. The connection came through the local Wheaton/ Kensington Chamber of Commerce. I was serving on the Chamber's Board of Directors. I learned about the M.U.M. food pantry and their service to the under resourced of 5 zip codes in Montgomery County. They also offered financial help to individuals or families that were in crisis.

Our church stepped up to the plate of collecting nonperishable food for M.U.M. I will never forget one Sunday when we brought to the service our collections that literally filled the stage of the church with cans of soup, bags of rice, boxes of cereal and a host of other edibles. It was an outpouring of generosity that cemented our relationship with this organization that continued, even when our church physically moved out of the Wheaton area.

So, what I wanted to propose to Eddie was that I would apply for Diane Schroder's position and since it was a part-time position, could I also remain part-time with Streams of Hope until I could fully retire at the end of 2012-six months away. Of course, that would be contingent of being hired by M.U.M. He instantly agreed to that proposal.

After going through the application process again I had to dust off my resume and go through a series of interviews. I was hired to begin officially after Memorial Day weekend 2011. I spent the month of May being trained by Ms. Schroder. I learned that in addition to the food pantry, M.U.M. supplied funds in five zip codes for those who were facing eviction, utility disconnection or unable to afford prescriptions. And my responsibilities required me to oversee the generation of funds for this benevolence. Because of my weakness in administration, the M.U.M. board hired a woman named Margaret Safal to pick up the slack.

Margaret was unable to start immediately because her husband had scheduled a cruise for the two of them. She proposed that a lady she had great confidence in would fill in for her until she returned. That fill-in was Sylvia Correa. Wonderfully, Sylvia was fluent in Spanish which was extremely helpful since so many of our clients were Hispanic. She was truly a Godsend. And her long experience in serving in nonprofits instantly proved to be valuable. When Margaret returned it was agreed that Sylvia and Margaret would both share the workload. Both were so needed.

I discovered early on that God had an additional reason to bring Sylvia on board. She was spiritually very hungry and teachable. When her parents brought her and her brother over to the U.S. from the Dominican Republic they were just children. When she was eight years old her parents were tragically killed in an automobile accident which meant that she was raised by nuns in an orphanage.

When she turned eighteen, she married a young soldier. The marriage lasted five years and ended in divorce. Because of the divorce, the Catholic church denied her the eucharist and in her hurt she walked away from the church and basically had felt estranged from God as she understood him. Now she was in her sixties.

As we worked side by side in the tiny M.U.M. office, we talked incessantly about scripture, prayer, and a relationship with God through Jesus. She began to read her Bible and would come in with very salient questions and eventually I was able to share with her how she too could know Jesus personally. She trusted Christ and was baptized at the local Methodist church whose pastor, Adam Snell, had become a volunteer every week at our food pantry. [See the conclusion of Sylvia's story in the section entitled "The Rest of the Story" at the end of this book.]

Having spent most of my career in the church, and particularly being on staff, I suffered what many "full-time" ministers struggle with- isolation from the world. How do you meaningfully connect with nonbelievers? I tended to develop we/them mentality. I sometimes even perceived them as a threat.

Being at M.U.M. allowed me to break past that barrier and I even came to appreciate individuals outside the church as blessings. No, they didn't buy into my world view or belief system, but they proved to be assets to good causes as they gave of their time and resources. And they were, for the most part, good friends even when I couldn't go to the levels of communication with them as I had the friends in church.

20/20 Hindsight

God calls his children to be salt and light. It takes work to get out from under the bushel and to spill out of the shaker. But it is so worth it.

It All Began When…

Elizabeth

My cell phone rang one Sunday night in October of 2019. Elizabeth was on the other end. She was crying as she told Becky and I that her life had come to a point when she felt utterly empty. She had no direction. She was calling from Tucson where she had relocated, over a year prior.

Elizabeth had married a young man named Jeff about two years after we had left Chicago. It was a rushed wedding performed in a lovely park right at sunset. They were expecting their first child and wanted him to have the benefit of a married mom and dad.

That marriage was quite rocky and at one point they had come to live in our basement apartment. During that time, they gave birth to their second child, Chase. But after his birth, they moved back to Illinois. About a year after they returned to Illinois, the marriage fell apart. Now she was a single mom with two young boys.

The distance between Elizabeth and us was not just geographical; it was very strained, though we worked hard to keep the communication lines open. We had learned through her ex-husband and her Facebook posting that she was now seeing someone new, and that new person was a young woman.

Eventually that relationship came to marriage. We were not invited to the nuptials. We were disturbed by her choice but also relieved that we were never invited to affirm that decision. On several occasions we visited with and even vacationed with Elizabeth and Torrie. When they traveled to Maryland to see us, they respectfully chose to stay in a local motel. When we met them in Kentucky to tour Noah's Ark, we had an enjoyable time but maintained respectful distances. Even when we went to visit them in their home in Crystal Lake, we chose to not stay in their home.

Included in that Chicago visit, we attended the church that had performed the wedding for Elizabeth and Torrie. The pastor was warm and welcoming, and he told us how much he was impressed by our daughter's faith. I didn't ask for an explanation, but I speculated that he meant her knowledge of the Bible.

It reminded me of her ex-husbands comment to me when I was able, over the phone, to share the gospel with him (it was after their break-up). He said, "I remember Elizabeth telling me this when we were married."

It was not long after our Noah's Ark visit that Elizabeth told us that she and Torrie were going to move to Tucson. They had even rented a house together. Since her job gave her latitude for working at home, she wanted to leave the frigid world of winter in the north. Early on in her marriage to Jeff, they had lived in Phoenix.

But when the time came for the move, Torrie decided that she not only didn't want to move west, but she also no longer wanted to be married to Elizabeth. The relationship Becky and I had so gingerly managed for five years was now mute. We had worked carefully to be accepting even though we truly did not approve of their choice. The ending of that relationship gave Elizabeth even more incentive to leave Illinois.

It had been 18 months after her move west, that the October phone call came. Breathing a silent prayer for help we went to the only thing we were comfortable talking about, Jesus. Her tears and anxiety about her life temporarily subsided as she engaged us positively as we shared with her how a relationship with Him was what she needed. I remember quoting His words "Come to me, all who are weary and burdened, and I will give you rest." (Matthew 11:28) Pastor Eddie had just preached on that invitation that morning. She volunteered that she had quite recently read that very passage herself. (She was reading the Bible!)

The conversation ended with us encouraging her to respond to Jesus' invitation and then to find a church. We recommended the one Becky and I had visited when we were there on Christmas almost a year earlier.

Two weeks passed and we prayed for her more intently than we had prayed before. We knew God was working in her life. Elizabeth's next call was her request that when we visited Tucson at Christmas that I would baptize her. Jumping ahead, that Christmas Eve when we attended the church she had chosen, the baptism took place in the jacuzzi that church used for such purposes.

That Christmas Eve was one of the highlights of my life. I reflected to that night 46 years earlier when God gave me His promise from Psalm 128. My children would be "like olive shoots around my table." While we were celebrating Elizabeth's baptism in Tucson, Bradley was clearly on a spiritual journey toward putting his incarceration and addiction in the rearview mirror. He was participating in a yearlong rehab program in Anderson, South Carolina. He had chosen to place himself under this program and from all we were hearing, he was doing quite well. My "olive shoots" were sprouting.

20/20 Hindsight

Proverbs 22: "Train up a child in the way they should go and when they are older, they will not depart from it." I do not claim to have been a great parent, nor do I believe this is an iron clad promise. But the general truth it espouses holds true.

It All Began When…

A Mauie Owie

We boarded the cruise ship from Honolulu to Maui. This was two days after we had left Tucson and Elizabeth. The sun was beginning to set and our cruise around the Islands had started. It was our second cruise. Some years before we had toured Alaska by land and by sea. It was fabulous. I had reservations that this experience would not even come close to our Alaska excursion. How little did I know this hunch was right.

The next morning, we were set to travel the Hana Road. It is a precarious winding trail that leaves those in the tour buses breathless. I was stoked to have breakfast and catch the tour bus to Hana. Across from the breakfast table I looked at Becky and said what I knew would extinguish our plans. "Honey, I think I am having a kidney stone."

Kidney stones were not new to me. My first one went as far back as my 59th birthday. Prior to this 2019 occurrence, I had ended up in the hospital having to have the doctor fetch the stone while they had me sedated. That had been the third one and prior to that I had found myself in a doctor's office throwing up and crying like a baby. None of the three occurrences had been at all easy or pleasant. And when I began to experience "the throes of childbirth," I knew we had to cancel the Road to Hana and get on the road to the hospital.

Fortunately, the hospital was right by the water that our ship was setting on. And fortunately, the emergency room doctor was a urologist. It didn't take him long to conclude that I was experiencing my fourth kidney stone. He admitted me to the hospital and promised the next morning to retrieve the "little demon," even in time to catch the ship before we sailed on.

The next morning, both the doctor and Becky came early. After thinking it through during the night, the doctor concluded that he didn't want to enter the procedure because, "You are a long way from Maryland, and should anything go wrong you would be stuck here and that could prove to be very costly and complicated." He suggested strongly that we head back home.

And we did. After visiting the local pharmacy to get painkillers and another prescription for nausea, given by the doctor for our return trip, we disembarked our ship and took a taxi to the Maui airport. One overnight stay in Oakland and then we touched down at the Baltimore Washington Airport at midnight, New Year's Eve 2020. Little did we realize this was the prelude to one of the most difficult years for everyone lying ahead.

We of course were disappointed. But there were several upsides. We dubbed the whole experience our "Maui owie." Fortunately, I never needed the prescriptions the doctor recommended. I still have it in my travel kit, just in case. We can laugh now that the only picture we took of Hawaii was the picture of our ship through the hospital window. And we count our blessing that we had bought travel insurance. And I can truthfully write Hawaii off my bucket list.

20/20 Hindsight

James 4:13-14 tells us, "Now listen, you who say, 'today or tomorrow we will go to this or that city, spend a year there, carry on business and make money. What, you do not even know what will happen tomorrow. What is your life?" You are a mist that appears for a little while and then vanishes. Instead, you ought to say, "If it is the Lord's will, we will live and do, this or that." Hawaii, the little I got to see in person and the other views from pictures, is truly beautiful. We don't plan to ever visit there again but we realize we have a much more beautiful country to see someday in our future.

It All Began When...

Taking on the Pandemic

On our flight back from Hawaii, Becky and I spent the time talking about the future, after all when we land in Baltimore it would be New Year's Day 2020. Becky's job was at the childcare center and preschool attached to the Food and Drug Administration. She was coming up for retirement with full benefits in the summer. I was at the point in my life that I had been to many times before. I don't like to label it as boredom, I would prefer to call it restless. On the positive side I was looking for some sort of new challenge. I guess I could best summarize it, "I've been there and done that." The problem was I didn't know what next would look like.

But I knew before the flight was over, I would be handing in my resignation letter to M.U.M.'s next board meeting late in January 2020. It was brief and to the point. "At the end of the year, 2020 I will end my time with Mid-county United Ministries." The board was responsible during the intervening time to find my replacement. They had a year.

There was a mixture of surprise and dismay. I felt deeply confident that I had made a good choice even though I still didn't know what I would do come January 2021. Becky was equally confident her retirement would come at the end of the school year in June. But there was no need to inform them this early.

The February M.U.M. board was all about how we should respond to the Covid pandemic. We knew we could no longer serve as a choice pantry. Being "choice," meant clients were free to come and select the items they needed. For some time, we had coupled the choice pantry with a delivery of food every Sunday afternoon at 4 locations in the community. One decision the board made at that meeting was to close our walk-in pantry and increase our food delivery at the four designated locations.

By March the number coming to the four locations had risen from 25-30 to 125-175 each Sunday. It had been an amazingly smooth increase. Unfortunately, we were no longer able to operate at all as a choice pantry but had to bag and distribute items as long lines formed to receive our help. Equally amazing as the demand increased so were the funds to help and the volunteers to do the work. All of this strangely satisfied some of my craving for a new challenge. But I felt content to leave my resignation in its place.

The March Board meeting proved to be our last in-person meeting. The thrust of the meeting was spent with the board members warning me about the grave danger I was putting myself in by going to the local stores to buy the essential items we gave away. Yes, I am diabetic; Yes, when I was 55 I had undergone a double bypass. I was on pills for high blood pressure. According to the news I was in the category subject to the virus. But I am stubborn. Wearing the mask, they required at Aldi and other stores I continued to do some of the necessary buying.

As time went on, I formed a strong opinion concerning my choice. I had learned that during the black plague, Martin Luther and his wife not only refused to run from the plague but boldly took the sick into their home to care for them. I adopted their thinking. According to Hebrews 2:14, "Since the children have flesh and blood, he too shared in their humanity so that by his death he might destroy him who holds the power of death-that is the Devil-and free those who all their lives were held in slavery by their fear of death." I was not afraid. My lifestyle varied very slightly during the pandemic.

When I learned in late September that the M.U.M. board had selected a new director, I set my transition off from M.U.M. to the first of November. The farewell party was not alive and in person. It was a Zoom party. And because it was a zoom party, we had viewers who participated from as far away as Alabama and Minnesota. It was truly a memorable and celebratory time.

20/20 Hindsight

The pandemic was a time of extreme fear; even people who I had believed were strong in their faith operated out of fear. I truly was not afraid. But I also didn't want to be foolish. 2 Timothy 1:7 says, "For the Spirit God gave us does not make us timid, but gives us power, love and self-discipline" One translation says the Holy Spirit gives us a sound mind. I believe in the face of fear we can advance with the mind of Christ.

It All Began When...

The Road to Retirement

We traveled by car to enjoy Christmas with Becky's brother, Blake Edwards and her sister-in-law, Vickey Edwards. We loved road trips. This one was particularly freeing. Neither of us had to feel the pressure of returning to Maryland to go back to work. WE WERE RETIRED.

Somewhere on that trip we remembered a trip south we had taken a couple of years ago. We had stopped in Virginia to enjoy an early afternoon dinner at a restaurant. It was good southern cooking. And it was in keeping with our policy when we travel not to eat in restaurants, we could eat near our home in Silver Spring, so we enjoyed eating there when we got away from home.

With full stomachs, we continued our journey down I-85 when gradually sleep began to be a problem. I had always said that you tend to get sleepy after a big meal because the food causes your stomach muscles to pull your eye lids down. That was what was happening to me until suddenly I heard a loud crash and a big crunch on the passenger side of the car. In my slumber I hit a car coming up on my right. I pulled over and jumped out and ran back to the lady in the Volvo.

"Are you alright?"

"Yes, we are fine." Then she continued, "Now don't you worry about this old car. It is just a piece of crap."

I looked and it was already in rough shape prior to my colliding into the front driver's side. She insisted that we drive on and not involve a police report. When I saw the extent of the damage to our Toyota (which was considerably more than the damage to hers) I concurred. The rest of the trip Becky had to climb over the driver's seat or sit in the back since her door was damaged and would not open. But it worked until we were able to get home and pay out of pocket for the repair.

We had lots of memories of trips to Upper South Carolina to see our grandchildren. We enjoyed going south, but we both agreed that we really had no longing to move back there.

I asked Becky, "Have you ever thought about what you would do if I should be the one to go first?"

She didn't hesitate; "I would go back to Florence."

I said, "Let's pass that by Blake and Vickey and see how they feel about that."

Over Christmas dinner they responded enthusiastically and suggested we do an afternoon drive around the area to look at potential housing. We were particularly attracted to the communities that were filled with houses called "patio" homes. We knew that should this move happen we really wanted something smaller and more manageable. Without the benefit of going on the inside we began to dream of living in such a house.

I believe before we got back to Maryland, in our hearts we had moved on to Alabama. Later, we met with Jason Jutila, a realtor in our church, to discuss listing our place.

In early August we drove back to Alabama to see if we could find what we wanted in what would be our 8th home. Based on our experience of house hunting in Silver Spring 19 years earlier, I thought it might take at least a week. But it didn't. The first day out, the fourth house we saw was it. Yes, it was a patio house with an HOA that would take care of cutting our future small yard. It had just come back on the market the day we saw it. We made our offer, it was accepted. We started back to Maryland, but not before we went out to eat at Rattle Snake Saloon. After all, we didn't have that back where we came from.

Again, there was a lot to do, starting with officially announcing our plans to leave Maryland and hiring Jason as our realtor. And with Jason came a long list of improvements to our current property, most of which he took care of. Our job was a mixture of packing and discarding what we did not want in our new place.

As we were deep into our plans to leave Maryland I came home one Friday afternoon to discover an email that drew me into a response. It was from Norton Antivirus informing me that they had charged my bank account $538. They instructed me that If I had not authorized that charge to give them a call and they would take care of it. Immediately, I called the number they provided, and a young man took the call apologizing for the mistake. He assured me that he could get the money back into my account, but he would need my cooperation.

Since I had not authorized this expenditure (in fact, as far as I knew I did not have Norton on my computer) I was very willing to cooperate. It involved giving him permission to access my laptop and my bank account. After an hour of watching him maneuver his curser around my screen and go into my account, I said to him, "You know, I haven't seen you put any money into my account, in fact you have taken over $4000 out of my account." To that, he said, "I am so sorry. If you will not use your computer or cell phone for the next hour, I will straighten all of this out." I knew then that I had been hacked.

I grabbed up my laptop and my cell phone and headed to my bank, about 1 mile from my house. At the bank I was informed that indeed, I had been hacked. They would close out this account. I was to go to the police and file a report. And it was quite possible that I would NOT be getting this money back.

I proceeded to the parking lot when my hacker called me on my cell. He was furious, "You did not do what I told you to do." To which I replied, "I absolutely did do what you told me. I have not used my cell phone or my laptop. I brought it to the bank, and they told me you have hacked me. If you will wait just a bit, I'm going to call you back." My plan was to get to the police station, file my report and have the police talk with him.

That plan almost worked except he beat me to the next phone call. He called again angrily accusing me of not keeping my promise to call him.

I proceeded with the firmest voice I could muster, "Do you know that you are a scammer, a thief, and a liar? I want to tell you something my dad used to tell me when I was a kid. In the book of The Revelation, the last book in the Bible, it says that 'all liars will have their place in the lake of fire.'

There was a brief silence on the other end, and he asked, "What does that mean?"

"It means you are going to Hell." There was a long pause on the other end, and it sounded like he was crying.

Then he said, "I don't really want to do this to people, but I live in New Deli, India and things are so bad here that I don't know any other way to make it. My dad is facing a medical procedure next week and I don't know how I am going to get the money to pay for it. Besides, out of the money we got from you, I only get $200." Then he took a defensive approach, "Don't you ever lie?"

"Yes, I have lied. But because I know that Jesus Christ through His death on the cross for me has paid for my sins, I do not have to face the consequences of what I have done. I am certain if you would turn your life over to Him, He would show you a way out of your difficulties."

Another long pause was followed with, "I am going to get this money back to you."

By this time, it was 5:00 P.M on the Friday before the long July the 4th holiday. I knew the bank would not open until the following Tuesday. During the weekend he called me several times assuring me of the return of my funds. He wanted me to call him on Tuesday after I opened my new account. No way was I going to do that.

Tuesday morning, I opened a new account. Surprisingly, on Tuesday afternoon the bank contacted me to let me know the money I had wired on Friday had been returned. Their question was, did I want it placed in my old account or the new one? I chose, of course, the new one. Becky and I were ecstatic that what posed to us a great loss had turned around. All the money was returned, minus $200.

At the same time, we were also preparing to do a tour of New England. That would eliminate 8 states from my bucket list and since we were this close, I might as well get them visited. Blake and Vickey made plans to join us.

By the end of September, the house was ready to be turned over to Jason. The movers had come and loaded up what we still planned to take. A friend of ours, John Yates, had committed to meeting the moving van as our Florence Realtor had worked it out for the haul to be stored until we could get it. Our closing our new home was set for October 15.

In the meantime, Blake, Vickey, Becky, and I were prepared to journey to New England. I will never forget how Becky and I sat on a low wall on the front porch of our soon-to-be former home and reminisced about all the memories we had there for the past 12 years. Tears of a sweet sadness welled in our eyes as we prayed together, thanking God for how he had blessed us and helped us as we lived there. It was the longest we had ever lived in one house in our years of marriage.

Then we were off the next morning to the sites of states I had only heard and read about during my lifetime. Becky and I both agreed the tour of New England was the perfect segway before Alabama. We had some grieving to do but the trip broke it up and made it easier. Plus, we found ourselves genuinely enjoying our new family.

But Blake and Vickey were just a part of our new family. This was the first time, except for our first year of marriage, that we had the responsibility of finding our church home. Prior to this, we went to the church where I was on staff. That had always been good, but now we had to trust God to show us where he wanted us to worship. We prayed.

The number one criterion in our hearts was that we wanted to be in a church that was racially mixed. That was truly the big takeaway from our time in Maryland. Vickey suggested we try Chapel, a church that met a little over a mile from our new house.

We had never attended Chapel because when we would come to visit, we usually stayed with Becky's parents and felt it was discourteous to visit other churches rather than the one where our host attended.

The first opportunity to visit Chapel came on the first Sunday of November. I knew that Chapel was considered a charismatic/Pentecostal congregation and certain stereotypes played on my mind about what the service might be like. Already I was thinking that this would not be the church.

When we entered the building, we discovered immediately that Chapel was friendly and racially mixed. The music was a familiar style, even though I didn't know any of the songs. But the best part of the first impression was the preaching of Pastor Bobby Gourley. It was so engaging and intellectually stimulating. We drove away talking about how much he had challenged us with his content. I mentioned to Becky that one of the members told me that he preached like that every week.

It was a complete departure from the stereotype I had anticipated and later that week I learned that Bobby was married to a lovely lady named La Toyia, of African-American descent.

We still wanted to check out other options. The next Sunday we attended a highly recommended congregation of 2000. It reminded me a lot of Willow Creek. We enjoyed the service which was very creatively done. But we both found ourselves thinking about Chapel.

We attended Chapel two more times. I had always advised new attendees at churches where I served to give a church three tries before deciding. Here I was taking my own advice.

There's one more thing about Chapel that was a huge draw on us. (To fully appreciate this, you may want to go back to chapter 5 and refresh your memory). The summer after Becky and I got married, Mike and Joan Lee and their girls moved to Florence. Mike was still working construction but through a connection to Methodist Lay Witness Missions in Alabama and a dynamic Methodist minister named Doc Shell, Mike and Joan had relocated to Florence for the purpose of helping start a new church. That new church was Chapel.

On the last Sunday of January 2022, Bobby concluded a brief series of sermons with the title: "The Power of One". He explained briefly to the congregation the story of the encounter Mike Lee (who was now with the Lord) had in Atlanta with Larry White. He said, "We owe Larry White a big thanks. We would not be here today had not God used him to lead Mike Lee to Jesus." Then he had Becky and me stand for recognition.

2020 Hindsight

My life verse is 2 Corinthians 2:14-16 "But thanks be to God, who always leads us in triumphal procession in Christ and through us spreads everywhere the fragrance of the knowledge of Him. For we are to God the aroma of Christ among those who are being saved and those who are perishing. To the one we are the smell of death; to the other, the fragrance of life. Who is equal to such a task?"

My answer to that question…."You Lord have made me equal to the task."

The Rest of The Story

Becky and I enjoy relaxing before sleeping each evening by watching on YouTube old gameshows that often predate our childhood. Often when there is a famous guest on the show, I have my phone close by to Google the name of the celebrity to find out what happened to them. Most have died, of course, but I can also learn about the end of their journey. Some of the stories are sad and a few are victorious.

Perhaps as you read the various accounts of God's working in our lives, you wish you knew "the rest of the story." Below are two that I want to pass on to you, the reader. Both are victorious, only because of Jesus.

The first is about Sylvia Correa who came to Christ at M.U.M. (You can read about her in chapter 28.) Sylvia passed away nine months after we left Silver Spring.

At Sylvia's request some years prior, I presented the following at her Celebration of Life Service June 4, 2022, Upper Marlboro, Maryland.

It was 10 years ago this month that I first met Sylvia. I was new in the director's chair of Mid-county United Ministries having been hired with the understanding that I was weak in administrative skills. So, the Board of MUM hired Margaret Saffel to be my administrative assistant. Unfortunately, Margaret could not immediately assume her responsibilities so she somehow found Sylvia to fill in until she could begin her duties. As it turned out it took both Margaret and Sylvia teaming together to keep me in line. Both had strong backgrounds with nonprofits and Sylvia had a long history of endeavors benefiting the needy. I was doubly blessed.

Sylvia and I often interspersed our time in the office with deep conversations. Not only did I benefit from her experience and knowledge, she benefited from my years in Christian ministry and seminary training. I found her to be wonderfully teachable. She was eager to know God and his word. She not only wanted understanding of what scripture taught but she proved very willing to apply what she heard. That was never more evident that when she publicly professed her faith by baptism at her new church, St. Paul's Methodist. She lived out what Jesus said in Matthew 18:3 "Truly I tell you unless you convert and become like little children; you will never enter the kingdom of Heaven."

There is one conversation with Sylvia that immediately came to mind when Denise, her daughter, called me and told me of her passing. Becky and I had invited Sylvia to go with us to the Lansburgh Theater in D.C. for the performance of "The Great Divorce." For those not familiar with this theological fantasy by C.S. Lewis, it was a story about individuals being invited into Heaven and their objections to the appeal. When one of the characters considered the invitation, he wanted to know if there were famous people in Heaven and he was told, "No one is famous in Heaven."

The next week as we processed the drama, Sylvia wondered why Lewis would have the character from Heaven assert that there was no one famous in heaven. In our highly celebrity saturated culture that was a predictable reaction. It is not that celebrities are banned from heaven no more than are the rich (Matthew 19:23) But like the rich, wealth doesn't gain favor with God; the famous don't gain entrance based on their popular appeal. Our only credential for entrance is our childlike trust in what Jesus has done for us. Religion is about what we do, Christianity is about what has God has done for us through his Son taking on Himself our deserved penalty for sin and our humble willingness to trust in that provision. Scripture says, "For by grace you have been saved through faith, and that not of yourselves. It is a free gift." (Ephesians 2:8-9)

So where is Sylvia today? I can tell you confidently that she is with Jesus. Listen carefully to some of Jesus' final words before his death, resurrection, and departure. *"Do not let your hearts be troubled; You believe in God, believe also in me, in my father's house are many rooms, that if it were not so, Would I have told you that I am going there to prepare a place for you? And if I go and prepare a place for you, I will come back and take you to be with me that where I am, you might be also."*

What is this room he is preparing for us who put our trust in Him? His words are somewhat lost on us but perfectly understood by those followers through the lens of their culture. They knew that when a man sought to marry a woman, he first established with her father the terms of the arrangement then he departed to his own home to prepare for the wedding. He informed his own father that he had found his bride and was ready to marry. From that point on, what would happen next was under the direction of the groom's father. The groom was to prepare for the wedding in the home of his father. He was to prepare the honeymoon suite in a room in his father's house and a house that he and his new wife would inhabit, usually on the father's property.

In the meantime, the bride was gathering her attendants waiting for the word that the time had come to join her groom. That time would come when the groom's father saw that all was properly prepared. (Matthew 24:36)

Jesus disciples understood. The relationship that they had begun with Jesus was to continue forever in the place he had prepared for them so they could be with him. Sylvia began her relationship with Jesus a few years ago. Where is she today? She is <u>with Him</u> forever in the place he had prepared for her.

Jesus continued, "You know the way to the place where I am going."

Thomas said to him, "Lord, we don't know where you are going, so how can we know the way?" I'm so glad Thomas asked that. It is the exact right question. Here is how Jesus answered it "I am the Way, and the Truth and the Life. No one comes to the Father except through me."

What happened to Wes Gestring the UC Riverside Student I talked about in Chapter 13.

Wes in his own words picks up the story at the point that I first encountered him on the California campus:

It all began one beautiful spring morning in 1978 as I was waiting for a lecture to begin on my university campus. Two men approached me and immediately I knew that they were part of one of two possible groups that approached people on my campus: either Scientology or some Christian group. They began to talk with me about the beautiful weather and then eventually turned the conversation to Jesus.

I looked forward to conversations with Christians because I knew they were weak people who needed Jesus as a crutch and that I enjoyed backing them into a corner with their beliefs. The two guys seemed interested to know what I believed about spiritual things so I shared with them my belief that Jesus was a good moral man whose teachings should be followed. Nothing more and nothing less.

I continued meeting with Larry, one of the men, for that semester during which time I was able to ask important questions to me. Since I was studying for a masters degree in soil science I had questions which were important to me, like "How can the Bible and science be reconciled?" We met together for that spring semester and then Larry asked for my phone number so that he could contact me next Fall. I gave him my number expecting to never hear from him again.

The following Fall I was surprised when Larry called so we continued to meet weekly. One autumn day Larry asked me to read an article entitled "Lord, Lunatic or Liar" by Josh McDowell. The article and it's argument backed me into a corner. It showed me that my belief that Jesus was just a good man whose teachings should be followed was not an option.

Did I believe that Jesus was crazy? No. Did I believe that Jesus was a liar? No. Did I believe that Jesus was who He said He was: Lord of the universe who loved me and died in my place for the payment of my sin? All the questions that I had about science and Christianity faded to the background and the question that rose to the forefront was "Who do I say Jesus is? Why did He come? What does it mean to me and what do I need to do? So, I realized that I was also a very weak person who needed Jesus as my crutch, and on November 15, 1978 I trusted Jesus as my Lord and Savior. My life took a dramatic turn that I would never have expected when I entered university almost six years prior.

I continued to Colorado State University and completed my PhD in Agronomy, was discipled further through Campus Crusade for Christ (CCC) on that campus, continued professionally as an Assistant Professor in Louisiana and then went as a volunteer missionary to Kenya and Zimbabwe, where I met my future wife, Beth. Larry presided over our wedding in 1987 and our journey continued to full-time missionary work with CCC in Lesotho Africa for 11 years and then with the Baptist Mission Board for 23 years in Lesotho and South Africa. Our ministry focused on evangelism and discipleship with young African university students while I served as a Professor of Soil Science on campus. Additionally, God led us into a ministry to strengthen African marriages.

As I look back on my journey, I can say that it all began not only on that spring day in 1978, but in a closet in 1979. Let me explain. After I made the decision to be a believer in Jesus, Larry continually tried to get me involved with other Christians. As I look back, I now know that he was concerned with my Christian growth and that I needed to be involved in Christian fellowship with other believers. He invited me to many opportunities for fellowship, but I always made excuses as to why I could not attend. Honestly, I lied to Larry with my excuses. My real reason for turning down his invitations was that I didn't want to be around Christians because I didn't really know them to be "normal" people. But one day Larry invited me to go the Magic Mountain Amusement Park with other Christians involved with CCC. I always wanted to go to Magic Mountain so I decided to go .... even if I had to go with Christians.

We were to meet in an apartment in the morning to leave for Magic Mountain. Larry was late so when we heard him arrive, we decided to play a trick on him and we all hid in a closet so that he might think that no one had come. As Larry rushed into the apartment the first thing he said was "Did Wes come?" When I heard this, I realized the love Larry had for me and that he really cared for me. It showed me his heart and his concern for my spiritual growth. His three-word question had a profound effect on me, unbeknownst to him. That began my journey into Christian fellowship, church, discipleship, volunteer missions and then eventually a life of ministry in Africa.

Larry was my faithful Barnabus, and I pray that I have been a faithful Paul to many Timothys in Africa who also found faithful men and women to teach others also. It began with Larry, then began with me, and is now beginning with others.

Non-conclusive Conclusion

Just as a story has a beginning, we usually expect an ending. I cannot provide you with an ending. Moses, who wrote the first five books of the Bible, some how was able to include his own death in his writings. I suspect his successor Joshua did the honors. I just turned 75 and according to Moses in Ps. 90, I am past my expiration date, but even Moses lived to 120. I do not anticipate 120 but, thankfully still going. And even if I pass, (which I will) that doesn't mean the stories end.

There is a book in the scriptures that has no ending. It just stops. It is the book of Acts. This book is like Acts. It has to stop but the stories continue. What God starts goes on forever. If I started something, at best it will end with me. But what God starting, using me, will continue long after I'm gone.

I appreciate your reading what I've written. I trust you have been somewhat amused, but I also hope you have been inspired to let God write His stories through you. That is the only thing that is lasting.

About the author

After earning a degree in Psychology and encountering the Holy Spirit at Myrtle Beach, South Carolina, Larry White set out on an adventure that included marrying his wife, Becky Edwards from Florence, Alabama. From there they journeyed to Southern California where they adopted two children. They served on the staff of Campus Crusade for Christ and Skyline Wesleyan. After a brief time outside of Greenville, South Carolina, they headed north to Chicago to serve on Staff at Willowcreek Community Church. Then, before retiring, he served in a Baptist Church outside of Washington, D.C. and directed a local charitable organization. Currently, he and Becky are retired in Alabama.

Question: Larry, how is it that you over the span of 40 years have been able to serve with such notable leaders as Bill Bright, John Maxwell and Bill Hybels?

Larry: The answer is right from the Bible: "Even a lizard can find its way into a king's palace." (Proverbs 30:28)

A possible subtitle

A collection of stories where God shows up in a life committed to living under the direction of the Holy Spirit.